ELGAR
VARIATIONS AND ENIGMAS

CORA WEAVER

ELGAR
VARIATIONS AND ENIGMAS

Copyright © 2015 by Cora Weaver.

Library of Congress Control Number: 2015907190
ISBN: Hardcover 978-1-4931-9343-1
Softcover 978-1-4931-9344-8
eBook 978-1-4931-9345-5

All rights reserved. No part of this book may be reproduced or transmitted in any form or by any means, electronic or mechanical, including photocopying, recording, or by any information storage and retrieval system, without permission in writing from the copyright owner.

Any people depicted in stock imagery provided by Thinkstock are models, and such images are being used for illustrative purposes only.
Certain stock imagery © Thinkstock.

Print information available on the last page.

Rev. date: 09/08/2015

To order additional copies of this book, contact:
Xlibris
800-056-3182
www.Xlibrispublishing.co.uk
Orders@Xlibrispublishing.co.uk
709653

CONTENTS

Acknowledgements vii
Introduction xiii

Chapter 1   The Weavers of Worcester 1
Chapter 2   'Dedicated to HJW of Leipzig' 9
Chapter 3   A Tangled Web 15
Chapter 4   'To Crown My Miseries . . .' 22
Chapter 5   The Colonel and the Actress 30
Chapter 6   Miss Weaver Leaves Worcester 42
Chapter 7   In a New Land 50
Chapter 8   The Wise Designs of Providence 56
Chapter 9   A Zealous and Energetic Quartet 63
Chapter 10 The Thirteenth Enigma? 70
Chapter 11 'Flotsam on the Fringe of Hell' 78
Chapter 12 Finale 87

Bibliography 93
Index 95

ACKNOWLEDGEMENTS

Ann Backhouse; David Beacham (All Saints Church, Worcester); Martin Bird; Bournemouth City Council (Cemeteries); Bournemouth City Library; Fr Brian McGinley (St George's RC Church Worcester); the Ives family (Australia); Eddie Oram; Peter Rose (NZ); Robin and Rosalie Palmer; Noeleen Sutton (NZ); David Weaver; the Elgar Birthplace Museum; the librarians at Wellington National Archive and the National Library of New Zealand; Patea and Hastings libraries (NZ); National Army Museum, New Zealand; Alex Miller (gravedigger and gardener, Prestbury Cemetery, Cheltenham); Portsmouth City Council (Cemeteries); Beverly Turley (Memorialisation Administration Officer, Cheltenham Cemetery and Crematorium).

I have to thank in particular Aucklander Noeleen Sutton for sharing her local and national expertise and Dr Eddie Oram for proof-reading.

Extracts and information from the following newspapers are all courtesy of the National Library of New Zealand:

Auckland Herald
Auckland Star
Colonist
Hawera & Normanby Star
Manawatu Herald
New Zealand Herald
Wanganui Chronicle
Wanganui Herald

All quotations from the *Elgar Diaries* are from Martin Bird's transcripts.

In original documents the surname Muller is sometimes Müller; the surname Sussman is sometimes Süssman or Süssmann. For consistency, Muller and Sussman have been used throughout.

The Value of Money

It can be frustrating not to know the historic value of money; for example, how much would £10 in 1880 be worth today? Using the website www.measuringworth, that £10 would be equivalent to £868.60 using the Historic Standard of Living (HSL) as a converter. Applying Economic Status (ES) as a converter, that £10 would be equivalent to £7,067. This discrepancy is confusing and distracting. Wages may be a more realistic converter. For example, in the mid-1860s an Indian Civil Service officer was well-paid at £300 per annum. A little later, in 1898, the average weekly wage for an agricultural labourer (some of the poorest members of a community) in Worcestershire was 14 shillings (14s), or £36 4s per annum. In December the same year, Elgar (married with one child, two live-in maids, and a large rented house) wrote to his friend August Jaeger that he could exist on £300 a year (£5 15s a week) but was only earning £200 a year. Bread at that time was 4d for a 1 lb loaf, and it cost 1d to send a letter. The half-year rent on Saetermo, the house Alice rented in Malvern in 1889, was £16 10s 9d. In 1881, an unfurnished house in London's fashionable Holland Park was 7 to 10 gns a week, while a house in a northern suburb of the capital was 10s–40s per week.

d = penny; s = shilling; gn = guinea (21s); 12d = 1s; 20s = £1

Abbreviations
BWJ (*Berrow's Worcester Journal*)
EBM (Elgar Birthplace Museum)

List of Illustrations   Page

Map of Worcester 2
84 High Street, Worcester 3
William Weaver, advertisement 4
Jane Weaver's grave, Worcester 4
6 Britannia Square 5
9 Albany Terrace, Worcester 5
3 Arboretum Road, Worcester 6
Elgar Advertisements 9
Konservatorium, Leipzig, 1882 11
Hotel Sedan, Leipzig 12
Gewandhaus, Leipzig, interior 13
Annie Groveham, advertisement 16
13 Welbury Drive, Manningham 17
8 Walmer Villas, Manningham 18
Registration of alien businesses, 1916 19
19 St Paul's Road, Manningham 20
Loretto Villa, Worcester 22
Temperance & Colonnade Hotel, Birmingham 23
4 Field Terrace, Worcester 24
Raikes family tree 31
Hazeldine House, Redmarley, Gloucestershire 33
Freestone Lodge, Southsea, Hampshire 34
Table 1: Summary of Napier's army and family life, 1875–1922 35
Darell family grave, Portsmouth, Hampshire 38
Stanley Napier Roberts 39
Norma Villa, Cheltenham, Gloucestershire 40
Stanley Napier Roberts's grave, Cheltenham 40
Apsley Crescent, Manningham, Yorkshire 43
Lizzie Groveham, advertisement 43
2 Apsley Crescent, Manningham 44
Lizzie Groveham, school prospectus 45
Lizzie Groveham, school concert programme, 1886 46
SS Ruapehu 48
Table 2, Ruapehu specifications 49
Mountnessing advertisement, Auckland 50
Mountnessing, Auckland 50
Bishop's Court, Auckland 51
Helen's advertisement for music pupils, 1886 52
Elgar's advertisement for music pupils, 1891 52

Helen Weaver, advertisement, 1886	52
School advertisement, Auckland, 1889	53
Gospel Temperance meeting, Auckland, 1889	54
Table 3, Helen Weaver in concert	55
Map of New Zealand	56
Queen Street, Auckland, c.1884	58
John Munro	58
Egmont Street, Patea, c.1920	59
Bank of New South Wales, Patea	59
St George's Church, Patea	61
The font, St George's Church, Patea	63
Nelson College, Nelson	65
Munro family, c.1905	66
Bank of New South Wales, Stratford	66
Newspaper report: Farewell to Mr and Mrs Munro, 1909	67
Joyce and Kenneth Munro, c.1909	67
Bank of New South Wales, Hastings	68
Lady Mary Lygon	72
Madresfield Court, Worcestershire	73
Kenneth Munro	78
Grey Towers, Hornchurch, Essex	80
Grey Towers under snow	80
Severn Lodge, Worcester	82
Church of the Sacred Heart, Bournemouth	84
Frank Weaver's grave, Bournemouth	84
Fr Francis Weaver's grave, Bournemouth	84
Lieutenant Kenneth Munro	85
Kenneth Munro's grave, Armentières	86
Memorial Hall, Auckland	86
2 Kingsview Road, Auckland	87
26 Pencarrow Road, Auckland	88
28 Lucerne Road gatepost: Elgar plaque	88
28 Lucerne Road, Auckland	88
Mater Misericordiae Hospital, Auckland	89
Munro family grave	89

INTRODUCTION

Miss W. is going to New Zealand this month—her lungs are affected I hear & there has been a miserable time for me since I came home.
—Letter from Elgar to Dr Charles Buck,
7 October 1885

For perhaps fifteen months during 1883–4, Edward Elgar was engaged to be married to Worcester-born Helen Weaver. The engagement was broken off, and he was heartbroken. She left Worcester and in 1885 sailed to New Zealand. For a century she was an enigmatic part of Elgar's life, until 1984, when new information about her was disclosed and further research into her life was undertaken. A further quarter of a century has passed since then, and more material about Elgar's first and lost love has become available. Into *Elgar: Variations and Enigmas* are woven facts already known about Helen and new information about her life in New Zealand during the five years between her arrival and her marriage: where she lived, her hobbies, and her employment. Many previously unpublished photographs appear, including some of her children, and more is known about her son Kenneth's military career. There is also a discussion about Professor Brian Trowell's hypothesis that Elgar met Kenneth in London in 1916, a theory that featured in Occasional Productions' 2006 documentary *Elgar's Enigma: Biography of a Concerto*. We are also in a better-informed position to decide whether Helen's voyage to New Zealand was reflected in the clarinet quotation from Mendelssohn's 'Calm Sea and Prosperous Voyage' in Enigma Variation XIII.

In the nineteenth century, an engagement was almost invariably the precursor to marriage, so some insoluble problem had interrupted the normal course of events. Within *Elgar: Variations and Enigmas* is a reassessment of the reasons for the ending of the engagement and a discussion of the two most compelling contenders: religion and money. These both feature beguilingly in the life of Elgar's brother-in-law, Stanley Napier Roberts, about whom little has been written. Napier's chequered life is examined as an intermezzo within this book. He may be regarded by some as an archetypal Chaucerian tragedy whose riches to rags story would not have escaped Elgar's notice.

In 1883, Elgar spent two weeks in Leipzig with Helen and seventeen-year-old music student Annie Groveham. Their mutual family circumstances of academic achievement, music, modest incomes, unexceptional houses, and a minimum number of live-in servants offer an insight into the class of people Elgar mixed with before his marriage. Annie has been the enigmatic figure of the Leipzig trio, but recently uncovered information about her life suggests why Helen may have fled to Yorkshire when her engagement ended. Annie reappeared fleetingly in Elgar's life in the early 1900s and corresponded with him and his daughter, Carice, several times during the 1930s. Annie's adult life was, like Helen's, distressingly affected by the Great War.

Elgar: Variations and Enigmas does not attempt to analyse Elgar's music. It is a tool for discussion, interpretation, and criticism. It is social history based on source material used by local and family historians: fieldwork, census and electoral rolls, parish records, wills, letters, diaries, shipping records, photographs, trade directories, monumental inscriptions, and newspapers. The most comprehensive single source has been the National Library of Auckland, which has digitised New Zealand's newspaper collection and much of its photographic archive and made the images available online. Invaluable images and information were discovered in libraries, record offices, houses, and cemeteries across New Zealand; in Bradford, Bournemouth, Portsmouth, Gloucester, and Cheltenham. London Metropolitan Archive, the National Archive at Kew, the British Library, and the Elgar Birthplace Museum have all made contributions from their archives and photographic collections, and Ancestry.co.uk has provided many family details. Worcester University library has been a great source of background reading; owners of houses in New Zealand where Helen lived, and several of Helen's distant relatives have also played a part.

Cora Weaver, 2015

CHAPTER 1

The Weavers of Worcester

In January 1884, twenty-six-year-old musician Edward Elgar was penniless and miserable. His wretchedness was alleviated occasionally by 'the little Music &c.' that he enjoyed with twenty-four-year-old Helen Jessie Weaver, the young lady with whom he was in love. Helen was the youngest daughter of Worcester boot and shoemaker William Weaver and his wife, Jane. They were married on Christmas Day 1839 at Claines parish church, three miles north of Worcester. (Elgar's grandparents were buried in the churchyard there a few years later, and as a boy, Elgar sometimes sat beside their grave to ponder over musical scores. His wife Alice recollected those moments in a diary entry on 12 August 1910: 'E. took A. for walk to Claines Church in A.M. & saw his relatives tomb & where he used to sit & read scores, years ago.')

The Weavers lived in Copenhagen Street, near Worcester city centre. Their first child, Emily Julia, was born in January 1843 and baptised the following month at the parish church of St Andrew. Ada Clara was born in 1846 (no record of a baptism has been found) and Louis Herbert in 1849. The family moved into Broad Street, where William employed seven men in his boot- and shoemaking business; Jane was a boot binder, operating the machinery that bound the boot together. Frank William, born in 1855, was to become a close friend of Elgar's.

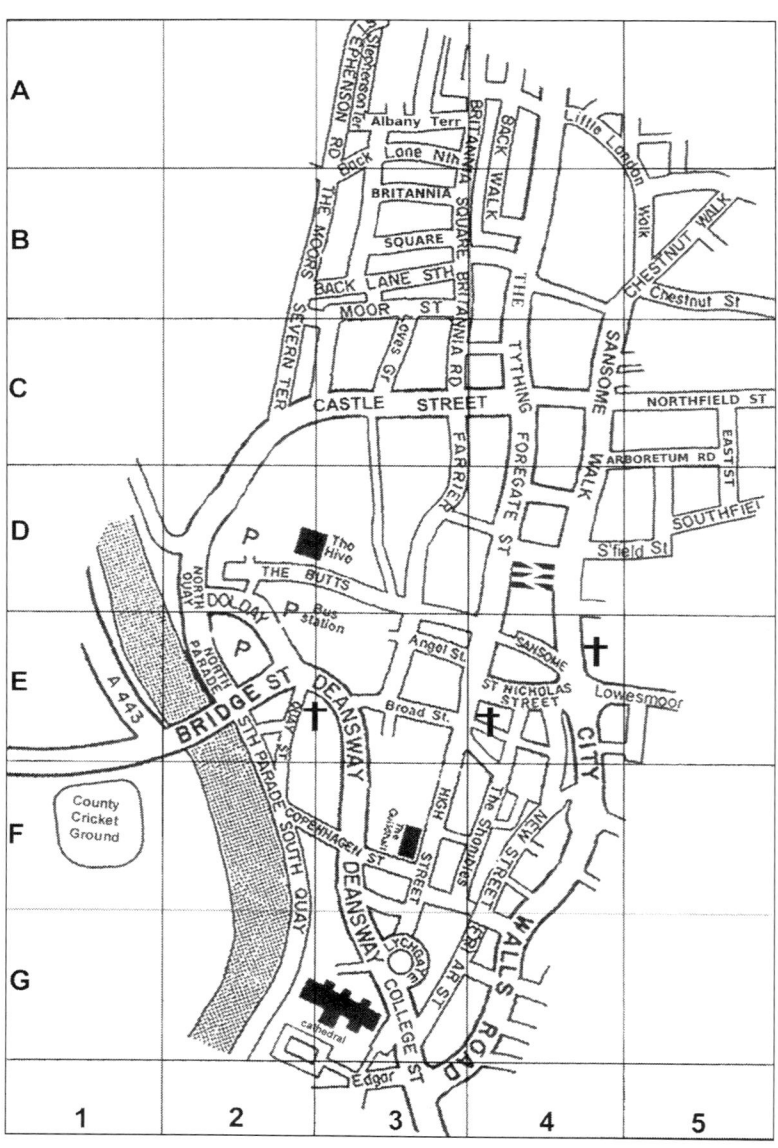

Map of Worcester

Albany Terrace	A3
Arboretum Road	C4
Archives (The Hive)	D2
Britannia Square	B3
Broad Street	E3
Bus station	E2/E3
Chestnut Walk	B5
High Street	F3
Stephenson Terrace	A3
Railway station	D4

Churches

All Saints	E2/3
Cathedral	G3
St George's RC	E4
St Swithin's	E4

84 High Street was in a prominent position near the Guildhall and only one hundred metres from the Elgars' music shop at 10 High Street.

A shrewd master shoemaker and businessman, William built up a thriving business and was involved in local affairs. He was an active supporter of the Free Library Movement and took a great interest in local societies for promoting the instruction and recreation of working men. The family and the business moved to 84 High Street, and Helen was born there on 27 December 1860. At that time, two-and-a-half-year-old Edward Elgar was living with his family two hundred metres away in Edgar Street, near the cathedral. In December 1863, Frank, Louis, and Helen were baptised at the parish church of St Swithin. Baptism in batches was common because it was cheaper.

> **CITY & COUNTY BOOT & SHOE MANUFACTORY,**
> 84, *HIGH STREET, WORCESTER.*
>
> # W. WEAVER,
> # BOOT & SHOE MANUFACTURER,
>
> Has always on hand an Immense
>
> ## STOCK OF BOOTS & SHOES,
> *INDIA-RUBBER GOLOSHES & LEGGINGS,*
>
> Waterproof Coats and Courier Bags, Travelling and School Bags, Boot Hooks, Button Hooks, Shoe Lifts, Boot Jacks, and every Article in the Trade.
>
> Cricketing Shoes from 7s. 6d. per pair; Servants' White or Brown Top Boots from 25s.
>
> The best guarantee of quality is the fact that an opportunity is afforded of Exchanging the Goods, or having the Money Returned, if required, any time within a month after purchase.

Emily married hop merchant Joe Longbottom by licence at St Stephen's Church, Paddington, in August 1867. Marriage by licence was sought by couples who wanted to marry in haste or privately without the publicity or delay of banns being called in their own parish church on three successive Sundays. The most likely reasons for a marriage by licence were that the bride was pregnant; there was family opposition to their marriage; that the couple did not share the same religion; or that they did not attend the parish church because they were non-conformists or Roman Catholic. Emily and Joe's was a civil marriage, conducted by a registrar rather than a priest, so with no religious aspects or affiliations. It was a brief, childless marriage; Emily died in May 1869 of muco-enteritis and was buried in Astwood Cemetery, Worcester. By 1871, Ada was married to Albert John Wilks, the son of a well-known local hatter; Louis was assisting in the boot shop; Frank was working as an auctioneer's clerk; and Helen was at school. For the past three years, the family had

Jane Weaver was buried in Astwood Cemetery, near her daughter Emily.

5 Albany Terrace (now no. 9).

lived higher up and further out of the city at 2 Belmont on Merryman's Hill in Mayfield Road, though the business continued to thrive in the High Street. The move may have coincided with Jane Weaver's ill health: indigestion, increasing breathlessness, loss of appetite, weakness, and a swollen abdomen. She would have been totally confined to bed by the time she died of chronic hepatitis in January 1873.

A little over a year later, on 25 February 1874, William Weaver married spinster school teacher Mary Mercie Awmack at Reading Register Office. Helen made her home with them at 84 High Street. Mary Mercie, Helen's stepmother, the daughter of a prosperous grocer, was a Quaker born in Wakefield, Yorkshire, in May 1849. By 1869, Mary had moved from Yorkshire to Raby House in Albany Terrace, Worcester, where she ran a school with the help of her seventy-four-year-old grandmother, Rachael Awmack. In 1873, they moved to a larger house at 6 Britannia Square, where they continued to run the school. It was a few doors up, at 11 Britannia Square that, between the ages of six and eight, Elgar had attended Miss Caroline Walsh's Catholic girls' school.

6 Britannia Square.

In January 1877, Helen's half-brother, George Bernard Dawson (usually known as Bernard), was born in Powick, on the south side of Worcester. He was not quite four years old when, in November 1880, his father died at 84 High Street of pernicious anaemia, aged fifty-nine. Frank was at his father's death-bed. He registered the death and made the funeral arrangements; William was buried near his first wife. William left his estate to his widow, including the rents from the two properties that comprised Belmont. He left personal mementoes to his children: to Louis, portraits of himself and his late daughter Julia; to Ada, another portrait of Julia; to Frank, a gold watch and chain; to Helen, his piano and two frames of Julia's needlework; and to Bernard, his writing desk in Russian leather. William gave Frank the option of taking over the family business, which he did. Usually the eldest son would expect to take over the family business, unless the testator mistrusted the abilities of that particular son or had overlooked him because of a personal conflict. However, by the early 1870s, Louis, who had learned the boot- and shoemaking business from his father, had moved to Birmingham and established his own business in Broad Street. Large cities offered non-conformists like Louis more opportunities to work and to worship. In 1876, he married eighteen-year-old Emma Blezard at a Unitarian chapel in Burnley.

After William's death, Mary and Helen spent some time with Mary's uncle Edwin in Reading, and Bernard went to Leeds to stay with his uncle Joseph (Awmack), a glass and china merchant. By September 1881, and financially secure, Mary and Helen were living in Britannia Square but shortly afterwards moved to a newly built house, 3 Arboretum Road.

The house was a short walk to the city centre and a stone's throw from where Elgar was living. In 1879, he had moved from the family home at 10 High Street to live with his newly married sister and brother-in-law, Polly and Will Grafton, at Loretto Villa, 35 Chestnut Walk (now No. 12). Several of Elgar's friends were also living in Chestnut Walk at that time: oboist Frank Exton; the Coupe family, and twenty-three-year-old pianist, composer, and songwriter Maud Eugenie Baldwyn (1854–1941). She lived with her father, Henry, a harpist and piano tuner; her brother Charles,

3 Arboretum Road (now no. 6).

who was a notable painter at the Worcester Porcelain factory, and a younger brother, Edgar, who was a pianist and violinist. The Baldwyns had a music shop almost opposite the Elgars' shop in High Street.

In his diary, Henry Baldwyn recorded that Maud was a lifelong friend of Elgar's and that Edgar had violin lessons with Elgar and played in the Amateur Orchestra under him for many first performances.[1] In 2011, a series of twenty signed letters sent by Elgar to Maud, Charles, and Edgar came up for auction. The earliest letter, dated 3 July 1889 from Field Terrace, shortly before his marriage, was to Edgar, regretting that the music lessons were to be terminated. The last letter, to Maud, was sent from South Bank nursing home on Boxing Day 1933. It is quite possible that Maud Baldwyn and Helen were acquaintances or friends and that Maud knew of Helen's close friendship with Elgar. Both young ladies were musical and both became music teachers. Also, in the early 1880s, the Baldwyn family moved to 3 Alton Villas in Arboretum Road, just three doors down from the house where Mary and Helen lived.

When Elgar Met Helen

When Elgar first met Helen Weaver and under what circumstances, is unknown. Their fathers were neighbouring businessmen with premises 150 metres apart in High Street; all their family members were educated; many were self-employed businessmen, and several showed a keen interest and ability in music. Elgar's father was a piano tuner, church organist, and purveyor of musical goods. Helen's father owned a piano and was probably the 'W. Weaver' who was recorded as ringing the bells at All Saints Church in April 1840 and St Helen's Church in December 1846, and the William Weaver who was ringing in February 1842 at St Helen's.

Helen may have met Elgar through her brother Frank's close and lengthy musical friendship with Elgar. Charlie Pipe, Elgar's brother-in-law, recalled how, in the 1870s, a group of waits[2] tramped Worcester's snowy streets carrying their music stands and instruments to play outside their friends' houses, 'amongst them Elgars, Leicesters, Griffiths, Box, Weaver, Coupe, and Exton . . .'[3] Frank and Elgar were violinists in the Worcester Amateur Instrumental Society and in the band at the county lunatic asylum at Powick. Both also belonged to the Worcester Glee Club: Elgar for several decades, Frank for a few years in the 1880s. During the years of

---

[1] Letter to the author from Rodney Baldwyn, DMus, dated 6 June 1989.
[2] Waits—a group of musicians who sing and play outdoors at night on special occasions, notably Christmas.
[3] *BWJ*, 24 February 1972.

his membership, Frank often performed at the club's many concerts, singing and playing his violin, usually in the opening number as part of a quartet with Messrs. Barry, Fleet, and Pedley. Frank had 'a light tenor voice of nice quality and fair compass'.[4] He was a member of the St Clements Victoria Band, a member of the Worcester Amateur Vocal Union and a tenor and cellist in the Worcester Volunteer Artillery Minstrels, of which Robert Surman was the manager. When, in February 1880, the city organist, Alfred Caldicott (who was also conductor of the Worcester Amateur Instrumental Society) gave a recital on the new Corporation organ in the Music Hall, Frank gave two vocal selections accompanied by the organ.

Apart from their respective religions, Helen and Elgar shared common values and interests. Helen was a musician; she was a pianist. She inherited the piano from her father, accompanied a piano student to Leipzig, and played accompaniment and piano solos in public. As well as their musical interest, the couple enjoyed poetry, both spoke German, and both enjoyed drawing. Elgar's humorous doodles are a common feature on his letters to friends. Helen went to fee-paying art classes: at sixteen she passed the second grade in model drawing at the Worcester Government School of Art. In previous generations, young people met largely at church-based events, but from the 1870s, theatres, concerts, dances, outings to the seaside, tennis, and public lectures comprised a marriage forum. Mutual values, background, education, social, and financial position, and geographic location were variable factors in partner choice among the middle classes in the nineteenth century.

---

[4] *BWJ*, 12 January 1878

CHAPTER 2

'Dedicated to HJW of Leipzig'

William and Henry Elgar ran a music shop at 10 High Street, Worcester. Edward Elgar began advertising as a music teacher in December 1884.

The course of Helen and Elgar's relationship can be traced through several sources: Elgar's own music; E. Wulstan Atkins's 1984 book *The Elgar Atkins Friendship*; the letters Edith Wood Somers wrote to Elgar and his daughter in the 1930s, and Elgar's letters to his friend and confidant Dr Charles Buck. Elgar's friendship with Helen developed over several years, probably because of their shared interest in music; she was almost certainly the 'Miss Weaver' who played a piano duet, *Le Cheval de Bronze*, with Miss Evans at the concert in Powick schoolroom in November 1878.

Between 1878 and 1883 Elgar dedicated several pieces of music to Helen. In April 1878 he wrote Shed no. 2 for his woodwind band, whose other members were Willie and Hubert Leicester, Frank Exton, and Frank Elgar.

9

The piece was dedicated to William Leicester but annotated 'Nelly Shed'. This is the earliest known reference by Elgar to Helen, who was then seventeen years old. She was sometimes Helen, sometimes Nelly. She was the 'Nellie Weaver' who Ann Elgar referred to in her scrapbook *c.*1883–4 and the 'Aunt Nellie' about whom Frank Weaver's daughter Maria Theresa said in 1984 that she 'forever regretted not pressing her brothers for more information about'.[5] In 1878, 'Nelly Shed' may have been no more than a friend's sister, but Elgar's enthusiasm increased. In October 1881, he wrote a new polka for the Worcestershire City and County Pauper and Lunatic Asylum entitled *Nelly*. Eight months later, in July 1882, Helen went to Leipzig and shortly afterwards, in early September 1882, Elgar wrote an orchestral piece that he entitled *Douce Pensée*, or 'sweet thought', probably about Helen. Just a few weeks later, on 15 October 1882, he wrote another polka inscribed '*H.J.W vom Leipzig gewidmet*' (dedicated to HJW of Leipzig) and entitled *La Blonde*. Other indications that Helen was blonde are that she later had a fair-haired, blue-eyed son and that her father had died of pernicious anaemia, which was most commonly suffered by people with fair hair, blue eyes, and wide cheekbones.

In the summer of 1882, when she was twenty-one years old, Helen was in Leipzig. It is believed that at that time she was studying music at the city's Conservatory of Music with seventeen-year-old Annie Groveham from Bradford. They probably arrived sometime after the summer term ended in July, in readiness for the start of the autumn term in September. There are several anomalies in their circumstances. Firstly, in a 1930s letter to Elgar's daughter (Carice Elgar Blake), Annie described Helen as her 'friend', but the age difference suggests that they had a different relationship; Annie was a child and Helen an adult. Elgar himself had called Annie the Infant, highlighting her youth as opposed to Helen's maturity.[6] Secondly, how might Worcester-born Helen have met Bradford-born Annie? Thirdly was Helen's age when she became a music student: Annie was seventeen when she began her studies at Leipzig; Helen, it seems, was twenty-one. Fourthly was Helen's apparent ability to pay for a musical education in Germany in the early 1880s.

It is more likely that Helen began her Leipzig studies in the summer of 1878, when she was seventeen, and completed them in 1881. When her father died in 1880, she did not inherit any money, so she may have been faced with a spinster's common dilemma: marry or earn a living, in her

---

[5] Letter from *Sunday Times* music critic Norman Lebrecht to the author (14 June 1984).
[6] Letter from Edith Wood-Somers to Edward Elgar (12 December 1932), (EBM, ref 2003.461 1058-).

case as a music teacher. Her stepmother was a teacher from the north of England and perhaps suggested that Helen should apply for a position as a music teacher at Mrs Groveham's school in Bradford, which is where she met Annie. Annie would not have travelled to Leipzig alone nor lived alone unless she was in supervised accommodation, and it is possible that Helen acted as her paid chaperone and companion.

The Konservatorium, Leipzig, 1882. In April 1843, Felix Mendelssohn, the music director of the Gewandhaus orchestra in Leipzig, founded a music school in the city which, from 1876, was known as the *Königliches Konservatorium der Musik zu Leipzig* (Royal Conservatory of Music of Leipzig). The music school's home was in the Gewandhaus (Cloth Hall), which was built in 1781; the teachers were the orchestra musicians.

Elgar was twenty-five when, on New Year's Day 1883, he left London for a musical experience in Leipzig. In his book, E. Wulstan Atkins says that Elgar consulted Frank Weaver about where to stay in Leipzig. In the 1880s, it was conventional for a suitor to ask the father of his intended bride for her hand in marriage. If it were denied, the marriage usually would not take place. Since Helen had no father and her eldest brother lived in Birmingham, perhaps Elgar told Frank that he would like to marry Helen and then asked Frank for his blessing. If Elgar had not made his intentions known or Frank had disapproved, Frank would not have suggested that Elgar should stay in the same hotel as Helen.

The Hotel Sedan, Leipzig, c.1900. Helen, Elgar, and Annie stayed here, as Alice Elgar confirmed in her diary on 31 May 1902: 'Left Dresden at 10 . . . had 3 hours at Leipsig, drove a little . . . Spent the time at Leipsig at Hotel Sedan where E. went when he went to Leipsig for 1st time—'

By the time Elgar visited Leipzig, the Gewandhaus was so old that its life as a concert hall was nearly over. The experience of concerts there was not a romantic one. English soprano Clara Novello (1818–1908) described the interior as 'small and frightfully painted in yellow, the benches arranged that one sits as if in an omnibus—and no lady and gentleman are ever allowed to sit together here . . . so that the women sit in rows opposite one another staring at each other's dress, which is celebrated for being as ugly as the men and women—the men standing round looking at you through an immense eyeglass the whole night.'[7] The young music critic Henry Chorley added that the men were 'crowded so thickly that anyone going as late as half an hour before the music struck up, ran no small chance of being

---

[7] W. Blunt, *On Wings of Song, a biography of Felix Mendelssohn* (1974), 176.

kneaded into the wall by the particularly substantial proportions of those before him, whom no good-natured wish to accommodate a stranger can make thin.'[8]

The Gewandhaus concert hall, which could seat five hundred, was made entirely of wood. It was replaced when a new concert hall opened on a different site in 1887. (Picture courtesy of the Museum für Geschicte de Stadt, Leipzig.)

Helen, Annie, and Elgar attended the free early morning rehearsals at the Gewandhaus and bought tickets for many of the evening performances. As well as the music there, they enjoyed music and poetry at the hotel. Annie recalled how they discussed Longfellow's prose and Elgar sent Helen a copy of *Hyperion*, which she loved because it was about student life. In January 1883, Elgar returned to Worcester, perhaps already engaged to be married. Annie Groveham may not have been told of the proposal, partly because it would have to be sanctioned by both the Weaver and Elgar families before it was made public. Annie perhaps never learned of the engagement because she was still a child when it ended.

By July 1883, Elgar had moved to 4 Field Terrace to live with his sister Lucy Pipe, and her husband, Charlie. Helen was in Worcester that summer, and on 23 August, Elgar wrote to Buck that, alas, his 'Braut' [fiancée] was

---

[8] Blunt, *On Wings of Song*, 176.

leaving on 3 September so he could be with Buck in Settle the following day. The use of inverted commas around *Braut* may imply that they were not officially engaged but more likely denotes the use of a German rather than an English word, particularly if the engagement had taken place in Germany. Until the 1960s, engagement was the formal and normal precursor to marriage; it was expected that marriage would always follow an engagement.

CHAPTER 3

A Tangled Web

Although Annie Groveham knew Elgar on and off over the course of half a century, little was known of her life between their first meeting in January 1883 and her letters to him and Carice in the 1930s. Born in Bradford, Yorkshire, on 18 March 1865, Annie Edith Bertha Groveham was the eldest child of commercial traveller John Chapman Groveham (1831–1882) and Elizabeth (née Pendlebury). Annie had one brother, Harry Ernest (1866–71) and two sisters, Mary Emily (1869–1950), and Mabel Ernestine (1876–1960). Elizabeth and John found time for charitable work, raising funds for good causes and accepting donations for distribution to the poorer classes. They also encouraged Annie to sing and play music. At a fund-raising event in the local schoolroom for St Paul's Mutual Improvement Society in 1873, two duets, *Come Home Father* and *Home to our Mountains*, 'by two little girls, named Annie E. Groveham and Miss A. M. Turner, were well applauded.'[9] Annie had private piano lessons, and in May 1882, when she was seventeen, won a Senior Certificate at the local Royal Academy of Music examinations. She then went to study music at the prestigious Leipzig Conservatory, where she also learned to speak and to write fluently in German. After she returned to England she took up a musical career that lasted until *c.*1908. Like Helen and Elgar, she taught music, and also played at local concerts. In October 1885, she played in a concert to raise money for the building of a Sunday school at her local church, St Mark's in Manningham when 'the brilliant pianoforte playing of Miss Groveham' was one of the prominent features of the programme.[10] She also helped to arrange the musical programme for the annual soirée of the Farsley Church Institute in February 1887. (Farsley is four miles east of Bradford.)

---

[9] *Preston Chronicle* (22 March 1873).
[10] *The Illustrated Weekly Telegraph* (3 October 1885).

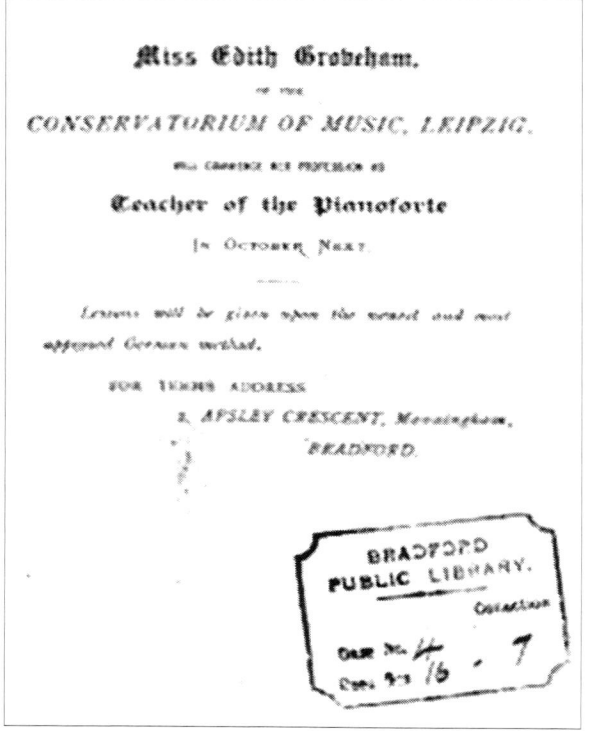

When Annie set out on her piano teaching career, she became 'Edith', as this flyer shows (West Yorkshire Archive Service, Bradford, ref. DB16/4/7). A young lady who advertised private music lessons in a Bradford newspaper in July 1884 charged five shillings per quarter for one-hour lessons. A similar advertisement in October 1885 charged 12s 6d per quarter for one-hour lessons or 7s 6d for half-hour lessons. Music teachers needed several pupils to earn a living wage.

During the early 1880s, the Grovehams lived a little over a mile north-west of Bradford at 2 Apsley Crescent, on the northern edge of Manningham. The German Muller family lived at No. 23, at the other end of the crescent. From the mid-nineteenth century, there had been a huge influx of economic migrants from Scotland, England, and Ireland who worked in the mills; professional wool traders like the Mullers came from other parts of Europe, notably Germany.

In March 1888, at the age of twenty-two, Annie Groveham married thirty-four-year-old Ernst Wilhelm Alphonse Muller in Manningham. Ernst, usually known as Wilhelm, was a clerk in a wool warehouse. Born in Bad Kissingen, Bavaria, he emigrated to Bradford *c.*1884 and in August 1885 the Home Office granted him British citizenship. His parents, and two brothers who also emigrated, remained German subjects. His father, Carl, played chess for Yorkshire. Wilhelm became a successful wool merchant making occasional business trips to Europe and America, taking Annie with him at least on one occasion.

Annie continued to play music and took to the stage. She belonged to the Bradford Amateur Thespian Society, and in December 1894 performed for three consecutive nights at the Theatre Royal in the drama *Diplomacy*. The part of Julian Beauclerc was played by A. W. Sussman, the son of wealthy paper merchant Alfred Sussman. In March 1899, at the annual entertainment to raise funds for the Working Girls' Club, held at St Luke's Schools, Manningham, Mrs W. A. Muller and Miss Groveham played the piano, while 'Mr. Wood Somers proved himself an accomplished vocalist in two sections.'[11] The significance of this information will become clear.

In a letter of 1938 to Elgar's daughter Carice, Annie related how she and Wilhelm went to a performance of *King Olaf* in Bradford, where they met Sir Edward and Lady Elgar. After that the quartet met up several more times when the Elgars were in the North. Annie particularly remembered 3 December 1908 when they all met in the Midland Hotel in Manchester after the première of the First Symphony. In the letters that survive, Annie did not mention that she had four children: Brünhilde (1889–1967), Ingrid Lucille (1891–1981), John Hermann (1896–1917), and Edith Florence Mary (1909–1993) or that Ingrid and Brünhilde became actresses. She did not say that by 1911 she was

After their marriage, Annie and Wilhelm lived in this modest house at 13 Welbury Drive, Manningham, where their first two children were born.

---

[11] *Leeds Times* (25 March 1899).

living in Pinner (Middlesex) with little Edith and wealthy paper merchant Alfred Wood Somers and that Wilhelm was not there; his business was still in Bradford.

Shortly after Ingrid was born, the family moved to a larger house in Manningham, 8 Walmer Villas. Alfred W. Sussmann lived at 18 Apsley Crescent, a lodging house approximately 100 metres away in an adjacent street.

Alfred Wood Somers was born Alfred Wood Sussmann, in Bradford, on 13 August 1868. His father, Alfred Sussmann (1818–84), was a German-born paper merchant, who took British nationality in 1853 and played chess for Bradford. When he died in 1884, his estate was valued at a healthy £15,748 3s 2d. His Bradford-based business was taken over by young Alfred who, during the 1890s, adopted the surname Somers in his private life, retaining Sussmann for business. (When his younger brother, William, became a member of the Institution of Civil Engineers in 1898, he was admitted under the name William Tom Wood Somers.) By 1909, there was no mention of Alfred Sussmann or Alfred W. Somers in Bradford. His disappearance coincided with Annie's disappearance from Bradford and the birth of her youngest child Edith in September 1909.

On 4 August 1914, England declared war on Germany and, following the German bombardment on Hartlepool on 16 December, there was a violent public backlash of all things German. This anti-German feeling escalated after 7 May 1915 when the *Lusitania* was sunk with huge loss of life. Many Germans anglicised their names; many returned to Germany, while others were interned as enemy aliens. In July 1916 the Board of Trade ordered that, under the Trading with the Enemy Act, aliens had to cease trading. Wilhelm's brother, Carl, who had not taken English nationality, had to wind up his electrical accessories business in Bradford. Germans in England came under increasing pressure, but it did not affect Wilhelm. On 7 June 1916, aged sixty-two, he left England for neutral America. The passenger manifest describes him as wool merchant William Alphonse Muller, 5 feet 6 inches tall with light grey hair and blue eyes; English, though of the German race. He gave his last permanent residence as Bradford, but his nearest relative as 'Mrs W. A. Muller Groveham', of Dorset House, East Grinstead.[12] She was using both her married and her maiden name. America joined the war in April 1917.

In April 1919, five months after the armistice, Annie and Edith Florence made plans to go to America. The ship's record has their next of kin in England as 'Mrs E. Groveham, Netherside, Woodbridge'.[13] Annie and Edith finally sailed to New York in July. On 28 November, Alfred Wood Somers also arrived in New York, and in December 1919, Annie, Edith, and Alfred sailed back to England together on the *Imperator*. The divorce records for the first quarter of the twentieth century held at the National Archive at Kew are thought to be complete, but there is no record of a divorce between Annie and Wilhelm; presumably she went to America to get divorced. On 21 January 1922, Annie Edith Muller, formerly Groveham, fifty-five, spinster, 'the divorced wife of William Alphonse

Life became increasingly difficult for Germans trading in Britain (*Malvern Gazette*, 15 December 1916).

---

[12] List or Manifest of Alien Passengers for the United States Immigration Officer at Port of Arrival, 16 June 1916; UK Outward Passenger Lists, 1890–1960.

[13] *Border Crossings: From Canada to US, 1895–1954*, record for Annie Edith Muller.

Muller', and oil merchant and bachelor Alfred Wood Somers, fifty-three, both of 10 Charleville Mansions, West Kensington, were married at the register office in Fulham[14]

In July 1913, Annie's daughter Ingrid married actor Charles Warburton. During the 1919–20 season, he performed at the Old Vic, and in August 1920, they and their two young daughters emigrated to New York. For a few years, Ingrid and her sister Brünhilde exchanged transatlantic visits. On 20 August 1931, the SS *Samaria* sailed from Southampton to New York carrying forty-one-year-old 'actress and decorator' Beatrice Gilmore. Persecution of anything or anyone German was probably why Brünhilde changed her name. The name change, signed at the Central Office of the Supreme Court of Judicature on 1 September 1930, confirmed that the former Brünhilde Muller, of Heaton, Bradford, was from that date to be known only as Beatrice Gilmore. She intended to stay in America permanently and several times during the 1930s visited her mother and stepfather at their home in Blewbury, Berkshire. Beatrice never married. She returned to England and died in Manchester in 1967.

In December 1925, Ingrid, still an actress, arrived at Southampton en route to see Beatrice. She returned to America in July 1926. Three months later, their father died in London, though his 'home' was this lodging house at 19 St Paul's Road, Manningham.

Annie and Wilhelm's son, John Hermann, moved to 10 Charleville Gardens with his mother and youngest sister, his mother's lover, Alfred Wood Somers, and Alfred's mother, Annie Sussmann. By 1911, John was a boarder at Woodbridge boys' school in Suffolk. His grandmother, Lizzie Groveham, and his thirty-five-year-old widowed aunt Mabel and her three young children, lived nearby. John was only seventeen when, in 1914, he joined the Duke of Cambridge's Own (Middlesex) Regiment as a private soldier. He appointed his mother, 'Edith wife of William Alphonse Muller',

---

[14] Details from the marriage certificate.

to act as his father's attorney for the execution of his will, indicating both that Wilhelm was not in a position to carry out this duty because he was in America, but that his parents were still married. John was initially posted to India and, at the end of June 1916, was sent to Egypt with the Egyptian Expeditionary Force. There he served as a second lieutenant and was mentioned in dispatches for his distinguished service. John transferred to the Royal Flying Corps and was temporarily promoted to lieutenant, so it was Lieutenant John Muller who was killed in action in Palestine on 31 October 1917, aged twenty-one. He was buried in Beersheba War Cemetery. John was awarded the Victory medal and the British medal, but it seems they were not claimed at the time they were awarded. In 1922, his Medal Roll Index Card was sent to 'W.A Muller Esq (father), c/o Mrs W.H Gilmore, 885 Park Avenue, New York City'. This suggests that in 1922, Wilhelm was still living in New York. He had lost everything. He had left his home and business and fled to America; his only son was killed fighting for England, then his wife divorced him and remarried. Despite these misfortunes, Wilhelm returned to England; on 24 October 1926, Ernest William Alphonse Muller died at 19 St James Road, Wandsworth, aged seventy-four. It was probably because of Brünhilde's change of name that it was not until 12 July 1934 that the administration of his estate, worth just £20, was granted to Beatrice Gilmore's solicitor.

In 1932, twenty-four years after their meeting in the Midland Hotel, Manchester, Annie wrote to Elgar, reminding him of the young girl in Leipzig whom he had called the Infant and thanking him for his music, which had lifted her spirits 'in dark moments'.[15] Edith Wood Somers died in Devon in 1946. Alfred Wood Somers went first to the Isle of Wight where his brother William lived. After William's death in 1947, Alfred sailed to America.

---

[15] Letter from Edith Wood Somers to Edward Elgar, 12 December 1932, (EBM, ref 2003.461 1058 -).

CHAPTER 4

'To Crown My Miseries . . .'

Elgar wrote to Dr Charles Buck on Sunday, 1 July 1883, in reply to an invitation to visit. 'The vacation at Leipzig begins shortly; my 'braut' arrives here on Thursday next; remaining 'till the first week in Septr; of course I shall remain in Worcester 'till her departure. After that 'twould be a charity if you could find a broken hearted fiddler much trio playing for a day or two.'[16] Elgar had stayed with Buck at the same time the previous year, immediately after Helen had left for Germany. He wrote to Buck again on 26 September 1883 to say that when he got back to Worcester everything was all right because his 'Deutsches Brief' [German letter] was waiting for him.[17]

Only two months later, on 11 November 1883, Elgar wrote again to Buck: 'Well, Helen has come back!! Mrs Weaver is so ill, dying in fact, so the child thought it best to return & nurse her; so we are together a little now & then & consequently happy . . .'[18] The happiness was short-lived. On 13 November 1883, Helen's stepmother died of pulmonary tuberculosis at the age of thirty-

In 1879, Elgar came to live here, Loretto Villa in Chestnut Walk (now 12 Sansome Walk) with his sister Polly Grafton. This was his home at the time he proposed to Helen Weaver.

---

[16] Quoted in Northrop Moore, *A Creative Life*, 101.
[17] Letter from Elgar to Dr Buck (EBM ref. 2006.388).
[18] Northrop Moore, *A Creative Life*, 101.

22

four. She was buried with her late husband in Astwood Cemetery. In her will she left Helen her 'screen and desk in one', half her electroplated articles, her best iron bedstead and its bedding, and a watercolour painting of a gypsy encampment by Worcester artist William Clark Eddington, who in 1885 lived at 14 Barbourne Terrace, a few doors away from Frank Weaver. All these items would be useful to a newly married couple.

On 13 December 1883, a month after the death, Helen travelled with her intended mother-in-law to a concert in Birmingham. Elgar was in the orchestra, and his *Intermezzo moresque* was to be performed. Helen and Mrs Elgar spent the night at the Colonnade Temperance & Commercial Hotel in New Street.

Ann Elgar's scrapbook contains this engraving of the Colonnade Temperance & Commercial Hotel, New St., Birmingham, with a handwritten note by Mrs Elgar saying that she and Nellie Weaver slept there on the night of 13 December 1883 and went on to Coventry the following day. The Colonnade was opened in January 1883. (Image and research material courtesy of the Elgar Birthplace Museum, EBM ref. 1556.)

On 14 January 1884, just two months after Mary's death, Elgar wrote to Buck: 'I was sorely disappointed at not going to town—but 'tis no use going there to sit in the house all day . . . I have no *money*—not a cent. And I am sorry to say that I have no prospects of getting any . . . it feels to me that the only person who is an utter failure in this miserable world is myself' and added as a postscript, 'P.S Miss Weaver is remaining in Worcester & the little Music &c. that we get together is the only enjoyment I get and more than I deserve no doubt.'[19] In this letter Elgar did not use Helen's name nor refer to her as his 'braut', as he had done previously. She was a formal 'Miss Weaver', suggesting that their relationship had changed. Perhaps the engagement had already been broken off, probably sometime between 14 December 1883 and 14 January 1884. For one or more reasons, Helen had not returned to Leipzig after the Christmas vacation.

By the time the engagement was broken off, Elgar was living here at 4 Field Terrace with his sister Lucy and her husband Charlie Pipe, as recorded on the plaque to the right of the door (see inset).

Why might the engagement have ended?

In a conversation with two of Helen's great nieces in June 1985 (Ethel Watson from Zambia, now living in Bedfordshire), and the late Ada Cawood from South Africa, the two ladies were not surprised by Wulstan Atkins's revelation about the ending of the Helen–Elgar engagement. They had known for the past forty years, they said, and the traditional family reasons were that 'He was too serious, too much like a professor; and then there was the Catholic element' (Mrs Cawood).

Breach of Promise

In the nineteenth century the ending of an engagement was a serious affair. Men proposed, women disposed, and a man might be guilty of breach of promise if he severed an engagement without overwhelming justification. A breach of promise case reported in the *Worcester Herald* (8 December 1883) concerned a young couple from Epsom. They met at Christmas 1879,

---

[19] Northrop Moore, 102–3.

and the following summer the lady accepted the man's marriage proposal. In November 1882, he wrote to her and said that he could never make her happy because he could never be happy himself, so they could never be happy together, and broke off the engagement. She took him to court and was awarded £700. A similar situation occurred in 1936. Miss May Lighterwood Hamilton, thirty-two, was engaged to be married to Derrick Casson, thirty. She gave up her job, bought a trousseau, and after he had seduced her, he broke off the engagement because he said he did not think they would be happy. The court awarded her £1,000 for breach of promise. Elgar's broken heart indicates that there was no breach of promise in his case.

Religion

Elgar's friend Ivor Atkins understood that the engagement ended because of religious differences: because the Elgars were Roman Catholic and the Weavers Unitarian. However, no written evidence has been found implying or confirming that Helen was Unitarian. Her parents were baptised and married in Anglican churches, and she and her siblings were baptised in Anglican churches. If Helen were Unitarian, she was unlikely to have become engaged to a Roman Catholic. 'It was in the "old" Dissenting sects . . . that marrying-in [marrying someone of the same sect] was most marked . . . These, Unitarians, Baptists, Congregationalists, Presbyterians, and Quakers, were the home of the nonconformist middle class.'[20] Thus Unitarians tended almost exclusively to marry other Unitarians, congregating in large cities such as Manchester, Leeds, and Birmingham, where they could find churches or chapels and people of their denomination, which is probably why Louis Weaver moved to Birmingham. Unitarians were usually well-off. They believed that education was the path to prosperity and the good of society and strove to promote non-sectarian education among all classes and both sexes. That Helen was as well-educated as any woman of her time might suggest a Unitarian background, but there were well-educated women across the religious spectrum. There is no reason to believe that Helen's Quaker stepmother disapproved of the engagement. Until 1860, Quakers would be excommunicated from the Society of Friends if they married out, but their rules relaxed. Mary married an Anglican so was demonstrably flexible in her view of intermarriage. Frank Weaver appears to have supported his sister's choice of husband. Although baptised and married in the Anglican Church, his wife and children all

---

[20] F. M. L. Thompson, *The Rise of Respectable Society*, 102.

became Roman Catholic, and Frank himself became a convert to Roman Catholicism a few years before his death.

In the early Victorian period, couples tended to marry within their own sect. There were more mixed marriages later in the period, particularly in the Anglican Church, which did not impose sectarian restrictions on marriage. Catholics were much stricter than Anglicans about marrying within the faith. '[The Roman Catholic Church] had long tried to insist on a promise, to be taken by a Protestant husband before a marriage with a Roman Catholic that the children should be brought up Roman Catholic.'[21] Charlie Pipe gave an account of his own conversion to Catholicism before marrying Elgar's sister Lucy. He said he became engaged to Lucy in March 1877, 'and was very much in love until July, when, owing to differences in religious matters, the engagement was mutually broken off. However, it was "on" again shortly afterwards.'[22] He had often attended the Roman Catholic Church, partly because he had some good friends in it, but largely because his fiancée worshipped there. After much thought, he took instruction and, after three years, was received into the Church on 15 August 1880 by the Jesuit priest Fr Humphries. He adopted the name Aloysius and gave up Masonry. But, said Pipe, after those three years, he had found no real difference between his old faith and his new one and, after a row with Fr Foxwell and his 'respected father-in-law', he had his name removed from the registers, reverted to the Church of England, and rejoined the Freemasons. He added that the reversion made no difference to his fiancée, and they were married at St George's on 26 April 1881. Following Charlie Pipe's example, Helen knew, when she took the almost irreversible step of becoming engaged, that her children would be raised in the Roman Catholic faith though she need not necessarily convert.

There may be some evidence that marriage to a Roman Catholic would have social implications, as F. M. L. Thompson observed: 'Who marries whom, without courting alienation or rejection from a social set, is an acid test of the horizons and boundaries of what each particular social set regards as tolerable and acceptable, and a sure indication of where that set draws the line of membership.'[23] It might be that Helen faced being 'cut' by some family members, friends, or an employer because she was planning to marry outside a religious and social set and chose to end the engagement. On the other hand, in an article entitled 'SERENDIPITY, or one thing leads

---

[21] O. Chadwick, *The Victorian Church, Part II*, 403.
[22] 'Memoirs of Charles Pipe', *BWJ* (16 March 1972).
[23] F. M. L. Thompson, *The Rise of Respectable Society*, 93.

to another . . .' Worcestershire historian David Everett wrote that it was 'fascinating to see how soon after the Catholic Emancipation Act of 1829 Roman Catholics were accepted into the establishment in Worcester.'[24]

It seems unlikely that there was any religious pressure from Elgar's family to end the engagement. Elgar's parents were Anglican when they married in 1848. Their eldest child, Henry John, was baptised in July 1850 in their local church, the Cathedral Church of St Michael, Worcester. Two years later, their daughter Lucy was baptised at St George's Roman Catholic Church, Worcester, following Ann Elgar's conversion. It seems that she never expected her Anglican husband to follow suit, and he did not prevent her conversion.

Elgar's Predicament

By 1884, most of Elgar's musical friends were established in businesses and professions. His younger brother, Frank, worked as a musician and piano tuner; flautist Hubert Leicester was a chartered accountant, and his clarinettist brother William was a master printer. Cellist Robert Surman was a successful surgeon dentist; oboist Frank Exton, who was living with the Coupes in the early 1880s, became a surveyor and land agent; Frank Weaver (violinist) was a shoemaker. Of Elgar's other friends, cellist Charles Buck was a doctor, and cellist Sutton Corkran, who worked for the Worcester Old Bank, was eventually promoted to branch manager. Elgar's brothers-in-law were also settled: Lucy's husband, Charlie Pipe, was a partner in a grocery store in Broad Street, and Polly's husband, Martin Grafton, had recently been promoted to manager of the salt works at Stoke Prior. Most of these men married, but none until their late twenties to mid thirties. Only Elgar and former waits musician William Box seemed at odds with the world. Professor of Music William Charles Box never married, possibly because he could barely make a living. He lived with his widowed mother in St John's, Worcester, and drowned himself in the River Severn at the end of March 1899.

On 21 April 1884, Elgar lamented to Buck that his prospects were about as hopeless as ever; he was depressed and unsuccessful. For people of his class and education, marriage needed to have a secure financial backing. It was to make sure that they could afford to have a decent standard of living that many middle-class men did not marry until their late twenties or thirties. Samuel Butler in *The Way of All Flesh* (written 1872–84) reinforces the importance of money in marriage. Theobald Pontifex, though penniless,

---

[24] Friends of Worcestershire Archives newsletter (Spring 2013), 7.

was delighted when Christina Allaby agreed to marry him. The engagement would be a long one, until Theobald earned enough to support a family. Given Elgar's income, Helen saw either a very long engagement or a marriage bringing 'housework, washing, cooking, quarrels with the maid, crying children and financial problems'.[25] Perhaps Elgar felt obliged to free her from the engagement.

Helen's Predicament

There may be a correlation between Mary's death in November 1883 and the end of the engagement just a few months later. After her stepmother died, Helen had no traditional spinster role looking after elderly parents or working brothers. Her six-year-old orphaned half-brother, Bernard, was in the care of his uncle Joseph and Aunt Anna Awmack in Leeds, and his future was in the hands of trustees.˙ There was no need for Helen to continue living in the large Arboretum Road house which, without a decent income, she could probably not afford to rent without taking in lodgers. The income from the rents and ultimate sale of the family's two houses in Mayfield Road were solely for young Bernard's benefit. Helen had to earn a living. 'It was the middle-class spinsters in families unable to support them in idleness who were perceived as constituting a social problem because of the scarcity of jobs of acceptable status.' [26]

Helen was an intelligent, emancipated, self-confident woman. By the 1880s, there were few remunerative opportunities for well-educated middle-class women except clerical work, nursing, or teaching. By the third quarter of the nineteenth century teaching provided middle-class women with more paid work than any other occupation. Well-educated women were needed to staff the increasing number of girls' schools; between 1875 and 1914, the number of women teachers rose by 862.1 per cent; men by 291.7 per cent. By the 1890s, one in six women was unmarried, and perhaps this is a reason why half a million went to search for new opportunities in the colonies.

Other Factors for the Breaking of the Engagement

There were innumerable and unusual reasons for women breaking off their engagement. In *Gracious Ladies: The Norbury Family and Edward Elgar*, Kevin Allen relates how Betty Norbury broke her engagement to Henry Little because she vowed she would never marry a man who swore; he had inadvertently said 'damnation' when he slipped over while ice skating.

---

[25] K. Gleadle, *British Women in the Nineteenth Century*, 182.
[26] F. M. L. Thompson, *The Rise of Respectable Society*, 92.

In 1876, Betty's sister Nelly (Eleanor) broke off her engagement to E. J. Webb while she was suffering with mumps, just three weeks before the wedding day. (Four years later, he became engaged to another young lady. Similarly, four years after Helen left, Elgar became engaged again.) There may have been several reasons why Helen and Elgar's engagement ended. Religious differences may have been one; Helen's need to be independent and earn a living another. Elgar's poverty and lack of progress may also have contributed. Elgar appears to have accepted that his engagement was permanently over, with no chance of reconciliation. He never wrote about his loss with bitterness, but more with resignation and self-pity, which suggests that the separation was inevitable.

* Bernard and his cousin from Reading, Sidney Awmack, were sent to Sidcot School, a co-educational Quaker boarding school founded in 1699 in Winscombe, Somerset. Bernard moved to Hoxton, East London, and in November 1905, he married twenty-nine-year-old Mary Ann Ball, a lithographer's daughter, at the Friends' Meeting House in Stoke Newington. They had no children. For several years they lived in Shoreditch, where Bernard ran his own company manufacturing electrical insulators. They finally moved to 'Powick' in Chelsfield, near Orpington in Kent, where Bernard died in June 1937.

CHAPTER 5

The Colonel and the Actress

'Felo de se'
Alice wrote in her diary on 22 December 1889 '[Sir T. Sidgrieves died] felo de se.' *Felo de se* means 'felon of himself' or someone who has committed suicide. Suicide was a malicious crime once punishable by a shameful burial at night with no clergy or mourners present and, centuries earlier, by forfeiture of property to the king. Something terrible must have happened for Sir Thomas Sidegreaves to take his own life. At the time of his death, he was fifty-nine years old with a young family. He had been a barrister at the Inner Temple and a magistrate, and for the past three years had lived at Melton Lodge, a large, detached Italianate villa along Wells Road in Malvern. He had a handsome annuity of about £1,200 a year, and all seemed well, though he had suggested to a friend that this was not the case. At breakfast time one morning, shortly before Christmas 1889, Lady Sidegreaves could not find her husband. She and her son and the friend who was staying with them searched everywhere. Eventually Sir Thomas was discovered in the garden lying dead under the rhododendron bushes. He had shot himself in the chest with the revolver that was lying on the ground beside him. At the inquest, held in his own house, it was discovered that Sir Thomas had lost a lot of money in speculative deals and believed that he and his family were ruined. He was buried in Malvern Cemetery. This is one nineteenth-century example of the impact of bankruptcy on men of Sidegreaves's social standing. Bankruptcy was a shameful infliction on a man, his family, and possibly his friends, colleagues, and profession.

Roberts and Raikes

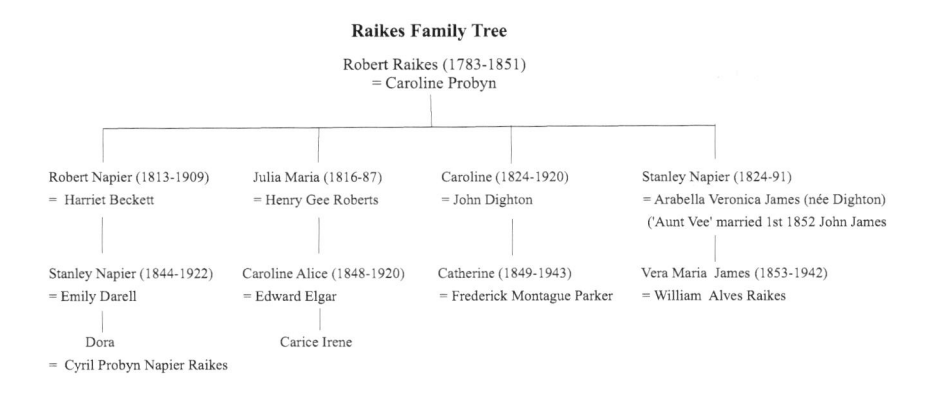

Raikes Family Tree

Robert Raikes (1783-1851)
= Caroline Probyn

- Robert Napier (1813-1909) = Harriet Beckett
  - Stanley Napier (1844-1922) = Emily Darell
    - Dora = Cyril Probyn Napier Raikes
- Julia Maria (1816-87) = Henry Gee Roberts
  - Caroline Alice (1848-1920) = Edward Elgar
    - Carice Irene
- Caroline (1824-1920) = John Dighton
  - Catherine (1849-1943) = Frederick Montague Parker
- Stanley Napier (1824-91) = Arabella Veronica James (née Dighton) ('Aunt Vee' married 1st 1852 John James)
  - Vera Maria James (1853-1942) = William Alves Raikes

Elgar's wife, Caroline Alice Roberts, was the only daughter of Major General Sir Henry Gee Roberts, KCB (1800–60) of her Majesty's Bombay Army. He was a doctor's son and grandson of William Roberts, president of Magdalene College, Cambridge, whose wife Anne's maiden name was Gee. Henry Gee Roberts joined the army as a young man 'and acquired both rank and honours more rapidly than generally falls to the lot of officers employed in the military or naval service.'[27] He began as a cadet in the East India Company in 1818, rose rapidly through the ranks, and in 1835 became a major in the Thirteenth Native Infantry. He was promoted to colonel of the Twenty-First Native Infantry in 1852 and created major general two years later. Sir Henry was thanked by Parliament for his military services, received the medal and clasp for Central India, and was made KCB in May 1859, the same year that he left India. He died on 6 October 1860 at the family home, Hazeldine House, Redmarley d'Abitot, in Worcestershire.

Henry married Julia Maria Raikes (1816–1887) in May 1838. Julia's father was Rev. Robert Napier Raikes (1783–1851) and it was his father, Robert, who had founded Sunday schools. Julia's mother was Caroline, daughter of Very Revd. John Probyn, archdeacon and dean of Llandaff. Julia's sister Gertrude married Sir Thomas Raikes Trigg Thompson, Bart., a vice admiral in the British navy. Her six brothers all joined the East India Company, and Robert, who became General Robert Raikes, is credited as 'the Father of the British Army'. Both the Roberts and the Raikes families were wealthy, well-educated, notable, highly regarded, respectable, and Anglican.

---

[27] *Cheltenham Chronicle* (1 January 1861).

Henry and Julia Roberts's four children were born in India. Albert Henry (1839–43), Frederic Boyd (1841–82), Stanley Napier (1845–1922) and Caroline Alice (1848–1920). Caroline was always known as Alice, thus avoiding confusion with her grandmother, Caroline Raikes, and Stanley was always known as Napier, distinguishing him from his uncle Stanley Napier Raikes. Like their father, Frederic and Napier made their careers in the army. Frederic joined the Bombay Artillery, served in Cawnpore, ended his career as a major in the Royal Artillery, and died at his home in Manchester Square, Marylebone, in February 1882. He granted the administration of his will to Alice and divided his personal estate, worth £884 4s, equally between Alice and Napier.

Wills and Property

Before 1870, single and widowed women (*feme sole*) could own money and property, but if they married, all automatically became their husband's to do with as he wished. If a married woman still owned land or property after her marriage, she could continue to do so but could not rent or sell either without her husband's consent. The Married Women's Property Acts (1870 and 1882) enabled women to inherit money up to £200 and property from next of kin independently of their spouse. However, legacies to spinsters or widows were often surrendered or reduced if they married or remarried so that money or property remained in the family from whence it originated. Often, wealthy parents put money or property into a trust, which provided a regular income to a woman independently of her husband; the capital sum, or the property, could only be redeemed or sold with the assent of the trustees, thus depriving a husband of any influence.

Until the Second World War, it was usually expected that the youngest daughter would renounce marriage to stay at home and care for one or both parents. After her father died in 1860, Alice stayed at home with her mother. Dame Julia made her will shortly after Frederic died in 1882. The contents were unexpected. Alice was the sole executor and inherited all the household effects including plate, china, linen, glass, books, prints, pictures, jewellery and furniture, the horses and carriages, and £200. Julia appointed her brother, Stanley Napier Raikes, and a 'cousin', barrister William Alves Raikes, as trustees of £2,500 which they were to invest, giving the income from those investments to Alice, so long as she remained single. If she married, the capital sum of £2,500 was to be given outright to Napier. Hazeldine House was left in trust to Messrs S. N. and W. A. Raikes, but it was Alice's to live in or live off the rents from it independently of any husband she may eventually have, and hers to dispose of as she wished in her own will. Julia left just £500 to Napier. However, in an undated codicil, she revoked the £500 legacy, reduced it to £300, but added a silver cup known as the 'Holkars cup'.* Ordinarily a widow would appoint a son, or a son's attorney, as executor, not a daughter. One would also expect that, if a trust be set up whereby a daughter had an income for life, or got married, the chief property, in this case Hazeldine House, would be left to the eldest son to keep in the family. Perhaps Frederic and Dame Julia appointed Alice, not Napier, as their executor, because Napier was absent indefinitely and Alice was very capable. Perhaps Julia left almost everything to Alice because she was protecting and supporting her spinster daughter who had, more or less, sacrificed any prospect of marriage. That does not explain why the £500 bequeathed to Napier in his mother's original will was reduced to £300, nor what was the significance of the Holkars cup. Was it because Napier was so wealthy that he did not need more money, or was he a wastrel who would gamble it all away? Dame Julia died on 30 May 1887 at Hazeldine House; her estate was valued at £7,946.

The Roberts's family home, Hazeldine House, Redmarley D'abitôt, in Gloucestershire (seen here c.2006).

The Colonel

After Alice was born in 1848, Julia and the three surviving children left India for Gloucestershire and took up residence at Hazeldine House. The two boys attended Cheltenham College where neither excelled in any way. Frederic was sent as a boarder in August 1852; Napier started as a day boy in August 1858 and seems to have lived in Cheltenham: the 1861 census shows Julia, Napier, and Alice, accompanied by a housekeeper, cook, and general servant at No. 4 York Terrace. From Cheltenham, Napier went on to the Royal Military College at Sandhurst and in 1863 joined the 104th Regiment of Foot (Bengal Fusiliers). As an eighteen-year-old ensign, he was posted to Parkhurst on the Isle of Wight, where the only notable event was that a private soldier stole his gold ring worth £2. It was recovered and the soldier imprisoned. In 1867, Napier was made second lieutenant and in 1873 an instructor in musketry; 1875 saw him promoted to the rank of captain. Napier received a medal for his service as captain with the Second Battalion in the Second Afghan War (1878–80) and was awarded a clasp for action at the decisive battle of Peiwar Kotal at the end of November 1878. In 1881, the year that the regiment was renamed the King's Liverpool Regiment, Napier was station staff officer at Dalhousie in Himachal Pradesh. He then served in India and Burma until he returned to England in the autumn of 1892.

In October 1875, Napier, then a thirty-year-old captain, married twenty-six-year-old Emily Catherine Mary Darell at St Edward's Roman Catholic Church, Windsor. He and Emily had two daughters, both born in India: Ethel, who died in infancy, and Theodora Mary (1879–1954), usually known as Dora. It was Emily's mother, Lucy Darell, and the rest of the family whom Elgar and Alice visited at Freestone Lodge on 25 May 1889 during their Isle of Wight honeymoon. 'Ventnor to Southsea to call Mrs. Darell &c.', Alice wrote in her diary.

Lucy Darell lived here at Freestone Lodge, Lennox Road North, Southsea, with her bachelor son, Edward. In 1881, Emily and Dora were also living here, having presumably returned to England while Napier continued his military career abroad. Ten years later Dora, then eleven years old, was still here.

It is not clear when Napier started to get into debt, but perhaps the 'a.w.b' that appeared in the Elgars' diaries thirty-five times between 6 July 1889 (two months after their marriage) and 17 September 1894 (coinciding with Napier taking up his position as lieutenant colonel on full pay) concerned Napier's profligacy. Perhaps 'a.w.b' meant 'argued with braut' because Alice had lent Napier money that he failed to repay after he received the £2,500 Alice forfeited when she married. She may have helped him financially on one or more occasions to preserve him from the same disgrace and fate as Sir Thomas Sidegreaves; to Roman Catholics suicide was so dreadful a sin that there could be no repentance. When she married, Alice knew that the full £2,500 that had been invested on her behalf would go outright to Napier. In which case, perhaps Alice married Elgar for money.

Table 1
Summary of Napier's Army and Family Life from his Marriage in 1875 until His Death in 1922

1 October 1975	Napier married Emily Mary Catherine Darell in Windsor.
January 1878–March 1889	Serving in Second Battalion Kings Liverpool Regiment in India, Afghanistan, and Burma. 1879—Dora born. 1882—Promoted from captain to major; Frederic died; Napier inherited £442.
9 May 1889	Alice Roberts married Elgar; Napier inherited £2,500.
1890	March—Elgar sold Alice's precious pearls.
1892	20 and 21 January—the contents of Hazeldine House were sold. October—Second Battalion prepares to leave Aden for England. 23 November—Napier visited Alice at Forli. December—Major S. N. Roberts promoted to Lt Col. on half pay.
1893	22 July—Napier went to lunch with Alice at Forli.
September 1894	The King's (Liverpool Regiment): Stanley N. Roberts, from half-pay, made Lt Col. of the Second Battalion on full pay. 1894—Napier met actress Lady Gipsy Rodgers.
January–March 1895	Napier and the Battalion were in Colchester.

1897	August—The King's (Liverpool Regiment), Lt Col S. N. Roberts was replaced and put on half pay. November—Napier retired on full pay of eighteen shillings a day. December—Messrs Isaacs and Wolfe filed for Napier's bankruptcy.
1898	17 June—'After lunch with Ellie Archdale to Exhn. At Knightsbridge. Back at 5. Emily & Dora to tea.' (Alice Elgar's diary)
1900	January—Napier became a discharged bankrupt. 31 August—'Chilly day. At. Vee, Willie Raikes & Napier's Dora to lunch.' (Alice Elgar's diary)
1902	9 July—'Napier & Mary came over from Hill Ash.'**** (Alice Elgar's diary)
1904	16 April—'A. & C. to Hill Ash by 1.29 train. Saw fields of daffs & shot rifle with Napier.' (Alice Elgar's diary) 4 November—'Napier came over to lunch.' (Alice Elgar's diary)
1905	7 June—'Wet gray day—Napier to lunch.' (Alice Elgar's diary)
1906	31 March—'Napier came over to lunch, left (bicycling) after tea.' (Alice Elgar's diary) 24 August—'Fine & warm—A. C. & May to the Holy Mountain—& Napier who cycled over to breakfast.' (Alice Elgar's diary)
1907	4 November—'Tried to make a scheme for Napier.' (Alice Elgar's diary)
1920	The four chief mourners at Alice's funeral in April were Elgar, Carice, Frank Schuster, and Napier.
1922	Napier died in Cheltenham.

In 1897, Napier left Aldershot and moved from army into civilian life. With his background of wealth and privilege, he would have expected, and have been expected, to have the finances to support a certain lifestyle. By the time he retired, however, he was in debt. Since he returned to England in 1892, he had lost almost £2,000 speculating on the Stock Exchange. There was worse. It was either while the Battalion was in Colchester or through an encounter at Paddington Station that Napier met an actress known as

Lady Gipsy Rodgers. It was reported in newspapers that she took several theatrical companies on tour around the country financed by Napier, who borrowed between £1,500 and £2,000 from money-lenders Jacob Isaacs and Jonas Wolfe, 'having no money of his own beyond his pay'.[28] The money would be repaid from her successes. Reports of theatrical entertainment in the London newspaper *The Era* record how Lady Gipsy toured the country with different theatrical companies but was never the star of the show. The earliest newspaper reports are in June 1893 when she appeared with J. E. Cowell's drama company in *Apartments to Let* and *Seaside Levées*. The same month, she appeared with Cowell in a farce, *The Married Bachelor, or Master and Man* when the programme ended with a burlesque *Beauty and the Beast*, in which Gipsy played Dewdrop. The following year, she toured with J. Pitt Hardacre's drama company playing the part of Lady Agatha Carlisle in *Lady Windermere's Fan*—in which part she was said to be very good. In September 1897, she starred at Exeter and Plymouth as Minerva in *Against the Tide*. *The South Eastern Gazette*, 1 March 1898, reported that Lady Gipsy Rodgers lived for some time at Maidstone, where she had produced one of her theatrical ventures.** They were a collective disaster.

On 17 December 1897, one month after Napier's retirement, Messrs Isaacs and Wolfe filed for bankruptcy. Napier had lost approximately £4,000 and had assets, apart from his pay, of only £86. He had been on half pay for much of the time since he returned to England, so presumably it was the bulk of the £2,500 he inherited when Alice married that had been lost on the Stock Exchange. The court determined how and when Napier was to pay off his debts, and the process of repayment began. Early in 1898, his application for a discharge was successful, despite the fact that his assets did not amount to half the £2,458 19s that he owed or that he had brought on his bankruptcy 'by rash and hazardous speculations'.[29] The terms of the discharge were that from his annual pension of £328, the War Office would pay £50 a year to the creditors' trustees in monthly instalments. After these deductions, Napier had £278 a year (£5 7s per week) to live on, which was barely enough for a retired man with a wife and a daughter. To put that into a lifestyle perspective: in December the same year (1898), Elgar, who also had a wife and a daughter, had complained to his friend August Jaeger that he was not managing to earn even the modest amount he needed to live on—£300 a year. However, Elgar had a financial safety net. John Drysdale suggests that as early as 1892, Alice's personal capital amounted to £5,000

---

[28] *The Times* (26 February 1898).
[29] *London Gazette* (16 January 1900).

in trust from the sale of Hazeldine House.[30] Together with the £442 from her brother Frederic and £2,000 in trust that she inherited from Aunt Emma in 1892, Alice's total capital was approximately £7,440; invested at 3 per cent, it would give her an annual income of £223.

In 1901, Napier, Emily, and Dora were living together in Twickenham. In February 1905, Dora married her distinguished first cousin once removed, Cyril Probyn Napier Raikes (1875–1963), the son of Major General Robert Raikes, at the Roman Catholic St Dominic's Priory Church near Hampstead. Napier and Emily may have separated after the wedding; in 1911, Napier, though still married, appeared to be living alone in Gloucestershire.

Emily died aged eighty in Portsmouth in December 1930 and was buried with her mother and brother in Highland Road Cemetery, Southsea. The memorial inscription indicates a Roman Catholic grave:

In Your Charity
Pray for the Soul of
LUCY DARELL
WHO DIED APRIL 30TH 1899

---

[30] J. Drysdale, 'A Matter of Wills', *Elgar's Earnings*, Boydell Press (2013).

R.I.P
JESUS MERCY MARY HELP
Also for
EDWARD DARELL HER SON
WHO DIED FEB. 14TH 1921
MERCIFUL JESUS GRANT HIM ETERNAL REST

Napier still had the support of his sister, as her diary entries show (see Table 1). Alice's last diary entry mentioning her brother was 4 November 1907: 'Tried to make a scheme for Napier.' Her 'scheme' may have been to bring him permanently from London back home to Gloucestershire. In a brief obituary in 1922, a newspaper reported that Napier had lived in Cheltenham for fourteen years before his death, making 1908 the year of his arrival. Gloucestershire was an obvious choice. Napier and Alice had been brought up at Redmarley, close to the county border; their father had been born at Chosen House in Churchdown, near Cheltenham; in 1911, Napier was living in Redding Lane, Churchdown. Also, Napier had been educated in Cheltenham, and there were other family members living nearby.

Napier continued his payments until his death, never eligible to benefit from a state pension because his income was too high, though it was low enough to attract tax relief. Following the general increase in prices after 1914 (food prices rose by around 130 per cent during the Great War) his standard of living would have declined unless he had another source of income, which is unlikely; at his bankruptcy, he had no savings or investments and had little chance of accumulating any except by inheritance. The last that was heard of Napier was at funerals. In March 1916, he attended the burial of his uncle Edward Dighton, who had been vicar of Maisemore (Gloucestershire) for thirty-eight years. Dighton's niece, Mrs C. K. Parker, was also there. Napier's final public appearance was alongside Carice, Frank Schuster, and Elgar as a chief mourner at his sister's funeral in April 1920. In her will she left Napier nothing.

Stanley Napier Roberts, from *Cheltenham Chronicle and Gloucestershire Graphic*, 15 April 1922.

Napier moved back to Gloucestershire. After a week's illness, he died on 9 April 1922, aged seventy-six, at this small, rented house, Norma Villa, (now Raleigh Villa) on the corner of Churchill Road and Asquith Road, Cheltenham.

Napier was buried in Cheltenham Cemetery (plot 1260 section A1). The grave was bought and a modest memorial erected the same year by his cousin, Catherine Parker, who also lived in Cheltenham. ˙˙˙˙

The inscription reads as follows:

IN MEMORY OF
COLONEL STANLEY NAPIER ROBERTS
8TH LIVERPOOL REGT
WHO DIED APRIL 10TH 1922
HIS COMPASSIONS FAIL NOT

* The Holkar dynasty ruled as maharajahs of Indore in central India until 1818 when, under the protectorate of British India, it became the Princely State of Indore. Today the Holkar Trophy is awarded to the winners of the Indian National Bridge Championship. Bridge is probably a mid-nineteenth-century Russian invention, which was brought to England in 1894 by Lord Brougham, who, it is said, learned it from some army officers in India.

** Lady Gipsy Rodgers was born Alice Ada Fricker in Poole in 1871. The 1901 census records 'Gipsey' Rodgers, a twenty-three-year-old actress (thus born c.1878), birthplace unknown. She was living in Southall, Middlesex, with a pair of actor brothers and her husband, Chatham-born medical student Maurice Rodgers, thirty-one, whom she had married in 1891. By the early 1900s, she was using her acting prowess to deceive, with a string of aliases: Aris Fitzroy, Alice Fitzroy Somerset, Hon Ida Falconer, Mavis Redfern, Irene Rodgers, Mary Cullam, Alice Rodgers, the Hon

Mrs Cholmondley, Jane Jones, and her favourite—Lady Mercia Somerset. Fraud, theft, larceny, and lies provided an income to support the lifestyle of 'a stylishly dressed lady, with auburn hair' (*Essex Newsman*, 19 September 1908). Gipsy was so good that Detective-Sergeant Humphries of West London described her as, 'one of the cleverest adventuresses who has been about in recent years' (*The Western Gazette*, 22 June 1917). She lived in numerous houses, mostly in Essex. In 1907, she was living near Clacton with six fierce dogs, three carriages and a manservant. The following year, she appeared in court accused of assault. She occasionally stayed at hotels with an accomplice; they were apprehended on more than one occasion for not paying and also for relieving the hostelries of their sheets and blankets.

In 1910, in the role of Lady Mercia, she visited Dr Crippen in prison to tell him that when he was released, he and his lover, Ethel Neave, could stay at her country home. In her memoirs, Neave recalled that after her acquittal, she was told that a woman of title was offering to care for her but described the woman as 'no titled lady at all, but someone who has since served sentences in prison for serious offences' (*see* Connell, Nicholas, *Dr Crippen* [Amberley Publishing, 2013]). 'Lady Mercia' later made money by publishing some of Crippen's letters. In 1911, she failed to turn up in court to hear a case of fraud against her. Nineteen seventeen found her and her two sons, aged twelve and fifteen, and her eighteen-year-old widowed daughter, Edna Gordon, guilty of stealing. Lady Gipsy served several short prison sentences, but in 1926 received six months for stealing from a shop and obtaining money by false pretences after convictions were proved against her in the Central Criminal Court, Rochford, Brentwood, Cirencester, and Haddingtonshire Sheriff's Court (East Lothian).

*** Hill Ash was the Gloucestershire home of Napier and Alice's uncle, Stanley Napier Raikes. It is said that Elgar and Alice did much of their courting there.

**** Catherine Parker (née Dighton) was a daughter of John and Caroline Dighton who lived for many years at Oak House in Newland, near Coleford in Gloucestershire. Caroline (née Raikes) was Alice and Napier's aunt; thus Catherine was Alice and Napier's cousin. Of the Dightons' six children (Mary, Julia, Maria, Catherine, Edward, Stanley, and Richard), Richard is the one most often mentioned in the Elgars' diaries. Educated at Southlea School in Malvern, he became a book publisher and moved to London, which is where he and the Elgars usually met. In her diary, Alice also mentioned the death of Stanley in Vancouver 'after much suffering' in February 1920, just two months before she herself died.

CHAPTER 6

Miss Weaver Leaves Worcester

On 21 April 1884, Elgar wrote to Buck, 'Miss Weaver is very well. I do not think she will remain in Worcester much longer now.'[31]

Where was she going and why? She was 'very well', so not leaving on account of poor health. Her engagement had been broken off; she had lost her stepmother and her orphaned young half-brother, Bernard, was being cared for in Leeds. It would have been a kindness to herself and to Elgar to leave Worcester and move nearer Bernard and other family members. Wulstan Atkins believed that she went to stay with Annie Groveham in Bradford and to teach. It is likely, therefore, that Helen went to teach music at Mrs Groveham's girls' school.

Elizabeth (Lizzie) Groveham (1839–1930) trained as a Pestalozzian teacher at the Home and Colonial School in Gray's Inn Lane, London c.1860–62. The Home and Colonial School was the foremost ladies' teacher training college of the day, and its alumnae were sought after. One advertisement, which appeared in *The Times* in 1879, read, 'A lady trained at the Home and Colonial desires an engagement as a resident governess in a boys' school. Acquirements—good English, arithmetic, French and Latin. Ten years' experience.'[32]

In 1864, Lizzie married John Chapman Groveham, had her first child (Annie) in 1865, and in January 1866 opened Bradford Girls' Middle School at 17 Drewton Street, Bradford.

---

[31] Quoted in Northrop Moore, *A Creative Life*, 104.
[32] *The Times* (26 June 1879).

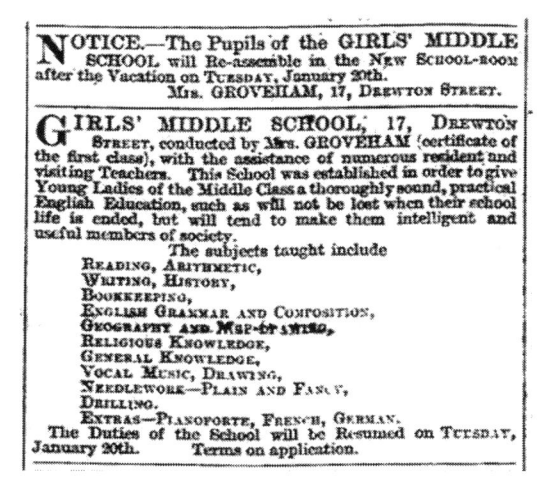

> NOTICE.—The Pupils of the GIRLS' MIDDLE SCHOOL will Re-assemble in the New School-room after the Vacation on Tuesday, January 20th.
> Mrs. GROVEHAM, 17, Drewton Street.
>
> GIRLS' MIDDLE SCHOOL, 17, Drewton Street, conducted by Mrs. GROVEHAM (certificate of the first class), with the assistance of numerous resident and visiting Teachers. This School was established in order to give Young Ladies of the Middle Class a thoroughly sound, practical English Education, such as will not be lost when their school life is ended, but will tend to make them intelligent and useful members of society.
> The subjects taught include
> READING, ARITHMETIC,
> WRITING, HISTORY,
> BOOKKEEPING,
> ENGLISH GRAMMAR AND COMPOSITION,
> GEOGRAPHY AND MAP-DRAWING,
> RELIGIOUS KNOWLEDGE,
> GENERAL KNOWLEDGE,
> VOCAL MUSIC, DRAWING,
> NEEDLEWORK—PLAIN AND FANCY,
> DRILLING.
> EXTRAS—PIANOFORTE, FRENCH, GERMAN.
> The Duties of the School will be Resumed on Tuesday, January 20th.   Terms on application.

At Mrs Groveham's Girls' Middle School, middle-class young ladies could extend their knowledge in the capable hands of resident and visiting teachers. (*Bradford Observer,* 16 January 1874)

Shortly before September 1879, the Grovehams left Drewton Street, and Lizzie took over Miss Margaret Macdonald's private girls' school at 2 Apsley Crescent in Manningham, a mile and a half uphill to the north-west of Bradford. Manningham's residents on the industrial west side included emigrant English, Irish, and Scottish mill operatives, while wealthy merchants (particularly German and Swiss), bankers, solicitors and other professionals lived to the north and east.

Apsley Crescent, a Classical and Italianate-style terrace, was built in Manningham in 1854–5. When the land was sold, conditions were laid down about the quality of the houses to be built there and that none should be used for industrial or business purposes. The modest-sized front gardens and lack of carriage space indicate a comfortable though not wealthy middle-class occupier.

In the 1880s, No 2 Apsley Crescent was advertised as Mornington House Ladies' Collegiate School run by Mrs Elizabeth Groveham. Despite being a conservation area, it is rundown and neglected, as this 2014 photograph shows.

One of Lizzie Groveham's visiting teachers was Charlotte Mason, one of the most notable and capable teachers and educational philosophers of the nineteenth century.* From 1880–91 she lived at 2 Apsley Crescent and taught part-time at Lizzie's school. Their close friendship, since their student days at the Home and Colonial teacher training college, is well documented. In 1881, clergyman's daughter and teacher Fanny C. A. Williams, thirty-one, was also staying with them. She became vice principal at Charlotte Mason's teacher training college for women at Ambleside, which attracted young students from as far away as Cornwall and Kent to train there. Helen may have met these two spinster pioneers of women's education, and their intellectual influence convinced her, in her early twenties, that for a single woman there were alternatives to marriage and domesticity.

> # Mornington House,
>
> 2, APSLEY CRESCENT.
>
> (LATELY IN THE OCCUPATION OF MISS MACDONALD).
>
> ## THE LADIES' COLLEGIATE SCHOOL,
>
> PRINCIPAL:
>
> ### Mrs. Groveham.
>
> The duties of the School will be commenced on WEDNESDAY, SEPTEMBER 10th, 1879.
>
> Whilst bearing an altogether private and select character, the School will possess the advantage of being conducted by trained and certificated Mistresses (First-Class, London), with an efficient staff of assistants and visiting masters. Instruction will be given upon the most improved modern methods.
>
> The Terms will be strictly inclusive, with the exception of Instrumental Music.
>
> Much importance will be attached to proficiency in Needlework. A Special Class for instruction in Fancy Needlework, in all its branches, will be held on Saturday Mornings.
>
> The Science and Art Classes will be held under the supervision of a regularly organised Committee. Examinations will be held in connection with the Science and Art Department, South Kensington.
>
> The pupils will be prepared for the Cambridge Local Examinations. Their progress will be tested by Half-yearly School examinations.
>
> A well-selected Library of upwards of one hundred volumes will be placed at the disposal of the pupils.
>
> The hours of attendance will be, in the Morning from 9 to 12, and in the Afternoon from 2-30 to 4-30.

Instrumental music was the only subject not included in the £4gns/term fee as this 1879 prospectus shows. (West Yorkshire Archive Service, Bradford ref. DB16/4/7)

If Helen went to teach in Bradford, why might she have given it up to go to New Zealand? Perhaps she could only get part-time work and needed a permanent position; there were plenty of employment opportunities for women in the colonies. Helen's decision also coincided with Annie Groveham establishing herself as a piano teacher at her mother's school. On the other hand, perhaps she went first to Manningham then on to New Zealand to distract herself from a broken heart. Elgar had taken himself off to Scotland for that reason; E. J. Webb went to America for the same reason after Eleanor Norbury broke their engagement.

> **MUSICAL MATINÉE**
>
> TO BE GIVEN BY THE PUPILS OF THE
>
> *LADIES' COLLEGIATE SCHOOL,*
>
> MORNINGTON HOUSE,
>
> Monday, July 26th, 1886.
>
> TO COMMENCE AT 3 O'CLOCK, P.M.
>
> **PROGRAMME.**
>
> Hatton ... Cantata ... "Flowers."
> Soloists:
> *Soprano:* Misses L. CHAPMAN and C. HALL.
> *Mezzo-Soprano:* Misses M. GROVEHAM and W. SMITH.
> *Contralto:* Misses CRABTREE and CHAPMAN.
>
> Moszkowski ... Pianoforte Duet ... "German Round."
> Misses RIESCHKE and M. SMITH.
>
> Reinecke ... "How it Looks in the Mill."
> JUNIORS.
>
> Schubert ... "Ave Marie."
> Miss MILLIE GROVEHAM.
>
> Kücken ... Duet ... "The Flight of the Swallows."
> Misses C. HALL and CRABTREE.
>
> Chopin ... Pianoforte Solo ... "Valse in A Minor."
> Miss RIESCHKE.
>
> Reinecke ... "Snow White."
> Misses B. AYKROYD and E. RYCROFT.
>
> Truschmann ... Trio ... "Te Prego."
>
> Dvorak ... Pianoforte Duet ... "Tu den Spinnstuben."
> Misses GROVEHAM.
>
> Keller ... Chorus ... "O Gentle Music."
>
> Faucheux ... Violin & Pianoforte "Romance sans Paroles."
> Misses MABEL GROVEHAM and MILLIE SMITH.
>
> Truschmann ... Trio ... "Das Veilchen."
>
> Mozart ... Pianoforte Solo ... "Fantasia in C Minor."
> Miss MAUD SMITH.
>
> Kücken ... Duet ... "The Happy Hunter."
> Misses CHAPMAN.
>
> Reinecke ... Songs ... { "To the Evening Star." / "The Peace of Night." }

John Liptrot Hatton is the only English composer featured in this musical matinee programme. (West Yorkshire Archive Service, Bradford ref. DB16/4/7)

On 7 October 1885, sixteen months after the end of the engagement, Elgar wrote to Buck, 'Miss W. is going to New Zealand this month—her lungs are affected I hear & there has been a miserable time for me since I came home' (from a visit to Settle that summer). This tells us three things. Firstly, Elgar was still clearly very affected by the loss of Helen. Secondly, if Helen's lungs were affected, it happened only after the engagement ended, so a lung ailment was not a cause for the ending of the relationship. Elgar's miserable time may have been because he knew he would never see Helen or hear her voice again, partly because she was emigrating but also because he believed she was suffering from a terminal illness. Thirdly, Elgar heard about Helen's imminent departure from a second or third party so was not in direct contact with her. She had moved permanently from No. 3 Arboretum Road because Henry Baldwyn recorded in his diary how he and his family had moved in on 1 January 1885.

Helen's Health

Bradford was famous for its factories and filth. There were soap works, abattoirs, carriage works, iron foundries, and factories that made almost anything out of iron; there were worsted mills and mills that processed every part of the manufacture of wool. It was the wool centre of the world. Manningham, on Bradford's outskirts, was a multicultural area and the retreat of the wealthy mercantile classes. Nevertheless it had its own dye works, cotton mills, worsted mills, and wool-combing works. A short distance south-west of Lister Park, steam-powered Manningham Mills became Britain's largest weaving and silk-spinning mill, employing up to eleven thousand workers. By 1884, there were two Anglican churches, one Roman Catholic, one Wesleyan Methodist, and a synagogue. For recreation there was a new library, and anyone could promenade in the extensive Lister Park, a large, green open space that opened for the public enjoyment in 1871.

Helen was in good health. A lung infection may have been caused by dirt particles; the high level of pollution emitted from the local factories was known even then to damage health. She may have been suffering from bronchitis, the symptoms of which are wheezing, breathlessness, a hacking cough, and mucus. A cough, phlegm, and breathlessness are also signs of pulmonary tuberculosis.

There are several questions about Helen's emigration that remain unanswered: whether she travelled alone or with a companion; who, if anyone, met her when she disembarked; whether she knew anyone in Auckland before she arrived; whether she knew there were vacancies for music teachers at the various schools. No evidence has been found to show that Helen went to New Zealand because she had family or friends there. 'People emigrated for many reasons. Some fled from religious persecution, some were convicts who were transported and some went abroad with the armed forces or for business reasons (but decided to settle abroad permanently). However, most emigrants left for economic reasons, especially poverty at home and the inducement of a new life abroad.'[33]

At 1.15 p.m., on 21 October 1885, the SS *Ruapehu* left Plymouth for Auckland. On board, travelling in the saloon with sixteen fellow first-class passengers, was Helen Jessie Weaver. There were eighteen passengers in the second class cabins, and the sixty-nine in the third-class cabins. The ladies

---

[33] M. D. Herbert, *Ancestral Trails* (1997), 576.

travelling in the saloon (first-class passengers) were misses E. M. Wilkinson, H. J. Weaver, H. S. Brodie and maid; Clarke; Snell; Mrs and Miss Marsden; and Mrs Hurst.

Under Captain Greenstreet, the ship reached Tenerife at 2.45 a.m. on 29 October and then sailed via Cape Town. It crossed the equator on 4 November. Light winds turned to a heavy gale, reducing the speed to ten knots, and they arrived at Cape Town on Friday 13 November at 10 p.m. They left the following day and had mostly good weather and fairly calm seas. There were a few northerly breezes but 'with this exception, the passage was accomplished in light winds, smooth sea, and pleasant weather'.[34] Helen arrived at Auckland's Queen Street wharf at 10.30 on the morning of 10 December 1885 after a journey of seven weeks, travelling from an autumn in England to a New Zealand summer.

SS *Ruapehu* c.1885 by Seymour, E. J., *fl.* 1885. (Photograph from Alexander Turnbull Library, Wellington, New Zealand, Ref: G-669.)

SS *Ruapehu*

The New Zealand Shipping Company was founded in 1872 in Christchurch and operated sailing ships between England and New Zealand. In 1882, the government offered a subsidy to build a fast steamer service, and five ships were ordered and built by John Elder & Co. of Glasgow. The *Ruapehu* was one of them and was built in 1884. All five steamers were expensive to run because of their high fuel consumption and limited cargo

---

[34] *Auckland Star* (10 December 1885).

space so were all decommissioned after only fourteen years. Ruapehu was essentially a sailing ship, with three masts and a single stack or funnel. She was launched in November 1883, and her maiden voyage was from London on 10 January 1884, via Capetown, across the Southern Ocean, passing south of Australia before reaching Auckland.

Table 2
SS *Ruapehu* Specifications
(from Plowman, Peter, *Passenger Ships of Australia & New Zealand*, Vol. 1 1876–1912 [Sydney: Doubleday, 1981])

Tonnage	4,163 gross / 2,655 net
Dimensions	length 389 feet ; breadth 46 feet ; draught 23 feet, 8 inches
Service speed:	13.5 knots
Engine	inverted compound two-cylinder steam engine, 600 HP
Propulsion	single screw
Accommodation	60 1st-class cabins; 40 2nd-class; dormitories for 200 3rd-class passengers: mostly south-bound emigrants.

* Charlotte Mason (1842–1923) established several schools in England from primary to tertiary. She believed and advocated that children should and could be educated despite their socio-economic conditions or heredity. When she was eighteen, Mason enrolled at London's Home and Colonial College for training women teachers but left after a year because of poor health. In 1863 she became the head of Davison Infant School, Worthing, but retired in 1873 due to ill health. From 1874–8 she lectured at Bishop Otter College, Chichester, but retired once again with health problems.

CHAPTER 7

In a New Land

Helen immediately found rented accommodation at Mountnessing, a large boarding house with a vinery, on the corner of Grafton Street and Wynyard Street opposite the Choral Hall.

> MOUNTNESSING, Grafton Road. —Private Sitting Rooms; Travellers and Tourists will receive every attention; beautiful view of the harbour.

Advertisement from *New Zealand Herald*, 10 August 1885.

Mountnessing in 1904 (Sir George Grey Special Collections, Auckland Libraries, 1-W1150).

She soon became integrated into Auckland's cultural life at the beginning of February 1886, attending a garden party, along with several hundred others, at Bishop's Court, the home of the Bishop of Auckland. By then, Helen was already earning a living.

Bishop's Court, Auckland.

In January 1886, after only a month in Auckland, the Visiting Committee of the Girls' High School had 'recommended the appointment of Misses H. J. Weaver and S. Young as music teachers';[35] and they started at the beginning of the term. Auckland Girls Training and High School, which accepted girls aged 9–19, opened in January 1877 in buildings rented from the Wesley College Trust Board in Upper Queen Street. The first principal was Sophia Sarah Stothard who, like Charlotte Mason and Lizzie Groveham, had trained as a teacher at the Home and Colonial College in London before going to New Zealand with the Church Missionary Society in 1860.

Learning music was not considered to be an important part of the school curriculum. In September 1888, a letter from the headmaster of Auckland College and Grammar School, Mr C. F. Bourne, was read to a meeting of the board of governors concerning this issue. Bourne said that both he and the headmaster and staff of the Girls High School felt that teaching music to girls was 'vicious' for two reasons. Firstly, the girls had to be taken from their classroom lessons to be taught individually, which was detrimental to their other work. Secondly, the noise from the piano was a great discomfort to the other staff and pupils. Some schools had banned music tuition altogether for these reasons.

By March 1886, Helen was also teaching music at Lower Glenside Boarding and Day School for Girls in Symonds Street, which was run by Mrs Alice Glover. When Mrs Glover died two years later, the effects of the school were auctioned off, the buildings were extended, refurbished, and improved, and the school reopened for the autumn term in February 1889.

---

[35] *Auckland Star* (15 January 1886).

Helen continued to teach there. She was also teaching music at Mrs W. J. Palmer's school in Carlton Gore Road.

> Auckland reputation abroad for musical talent has attracted to us another eminant instructress in music and singing from the leading school of Europe, viz., the Leipzig Conservatoire. We allude to Miss Weaver, whose notice appears in another column. We learn from those who have been fortunate enough to secure Miss Weaver's services that her aptitude to impart instruction is equal to her own skilful musical interpretation.

Almost as soon as she arrived in New Zealand, Helen advertised for pupils in the local newspaper. (*New Zealand Herald*, 29 March 1886.)

> MUSIC.
> MISS WEAVER
> Can receive Pupils at her Residence, Mount Nessing, Grafton Road, on Tuesdays and Fridays.
> Monday and Thursday mornings, at Mrs. Glover's, Symonds street.
> Monday and Thursday afternoons, at Mrs. Palmer's, Carlton Gore Road.
> ☞ Certificate and highest testimonials from the Leipzig Conservatoire, etc.

Helen's work in schools was part-time, so she set about advertising for private pupils. Perhaps it was Auckland's reputation for first-class music, its number of schools, and the desire for a good all-round education for boys and girls that lured Helen to New Zealand (*New Zealand Herald*, 11 March 1886).

> MR. EDWARD ELGAR visits and receives PUPILS for the VIOLIN, &c., in WORCESTER and MALVERN.
> Lessons also given in ACCOMPANIMENT, CONCERTED-PLAYING and ORCHESTRATION.
> For terms, &c. Address: 'FORLI,' Malvern; or, for engagements in Town,
> c/o MESSRS. SCHOTT & Co.,
> 2190] 159, Regent Street, W.

Elgar, like Helen, taught music in schools and advertised for private pupils (*Malvern Advertiser*, 8 August 1891).

> Prospectuses on application.
>
> # LOWER GLENSIDE,
> ## UPPER SYMONDS-STREET.
> ## BOARDING AND DAY SCHOOL FOR GIRLS.
>
> Principal .. .. Mrs. Young
>
> Assisted by an efficient Staff.
>
> This School has been enlarged and re-furnished throughout with all modern improvements.
> Every comfort and convenience provided for resident pupils.
>
> SUBJECTS OF INSTRUCTION:
>
> English Grammar and Composition, Literature, History, Geography, Science, Latin, Mathematics, Algebra, and Needlework—MRS. YOUNG, REV. R. H. GULLIVER, and Governesses.
> French and German—FRAULEIN HEISE.
> Music and Singing—PROFESSOR SCHMITT, MRS. YOUNG, MISS WEAVER, and MRS. KEOGH.
> Drawing and Painting—MRS. YOUNG and MR. BALL.
> Dancing—PROFESSOR FISCHER.
> Scientific Dresscutting—MISS BEWS.
>
> Musical Gymnastics daily without extra charge.
>
> Prospectuses on application.
>
> Term began 3rd June.

Helen taught music at Lower Glenside School for Girls. In 1886, the Girls' High School had eight regular staff and five visiting staff, Helen being one of the latter. Due to the depression of 1888, parliament withdrew its annual grant to the school, which closed, and the girls were assimilated into Auckland Grammar School. Helen probably lost her job at the reorganisation because she advertised again for more private pupils in May 1888 (*New Zealand Herald*, 31 August 1889).

In her leisure time, Helen sang and played piano solos, duets, and accompaniment at concerts, just as Alice Roberts did in the Gloucestershire and Worcestershire villages near her home at Hazeldine House. From mid 1886, Helen participated at numerous concerts, raising money for various good causes and church funds, regardless of denomination. She was particularly involved in two temperance bands, the Gospel Temperance and the Newton Olive Branch Band of Hope, choices that may reflect her mother's death from chronic hepatitis, which is often the result of excessive alcohol. The Band of Hope concerned itself with other social issues. One of its concerts began with an address on Woman's Rights, followed by music and singing. Another concert, held at the Sailors' Mission Hall to provide entertainment for sailors, started with 'devotional exercises' followed by an 'interesting address on the effects of drink'. Helen also attended earnest sermons at meetings of the Primitive Methodist Church, such as 'Wine is a mocker,' after which it was hoped some would sign the pledge.

> The fourth anniversary of the Sunday evening Gospel Temperance services was held in the Masonic Hall, Karangahape Road, which was well filled. Sir William Fox presided, and made touching reference to Father Damien's work amongst the lepers, and showed that by reason of the vastness of the evils flowing from the liquor traffic it was a worse plague than leprosy. Mr R. French briefly referred to workers who had removed, and the work done during the past four years. The Rev. J. H. Simmonds expressed his pleasure in being present, as he heartily sympathised with the work. He gave a brief address of a practical character. During the evening Miss Weaver sang a solo, the choir taking up the chorus.

Alcohol was just as much a social nuisance and destroyer of people in New Zealand as it was in England (*Auckland Star*, 15 July 1889).

Helen also joined St Sepulchre's (Anglican) parish glee club, which met regularly in the Symonds Street schoolroom. She could not have joined Worcester's glee club, which was solely for men, women attending rarely and by invitation only. Auckland's glee club meetings and concerts were a mixture of vocal and instrumental pieces, recitations, and readings. In June 1886, Helen and Mrs Palmer played a selection of piano duets at a packed glee club concert. Another concert, held in February 1887, started with a piano duet, *Bolero*, by Misses Dickson and Weaver, and the glees included *On the Sea*, *The Skylark*, *The Venetian Boatman's Evening Song*, and *The Victor's Return*.

August 1886 saw lengthy preparations for 'a grand vocal and orchestral concert' in the hall at St John's College, Tamaki, to raise money for the Diocesan Home Mission Fund. A local newspaper described how the roads were packed with private buses and carriages heading to the concert and how the hall was beautifully decorated with flowers, evergreens, and flags. The conductor was Herr Louis Tutschka; the accompanists Misses H. Weaver and C. Wright. There were vocal solos; songs by the twenty-three-strong school choir; pieces by the ten-piece orchestra; a violin duet; violin, cello, and clarinet solos; and the first part ended with Helen's piano solo, *Valse in E Minor*.

Table 3
Helen Weaver in Concert

1886	June, Glee Club, Mrs Palmer and Miss Weaver, selection of piano duets
1886	August, Diocesan Home Mission Fund, Misses H. Weaver and C. Wright, accompanists Miss Weaver, piano solo, Valse in E Minor
1887	February, Glee Club, Misses Dickson and Weaver, piano duet, 'Bolero'
1887	May, Symonds Street Church members, Miss Weaver, piano solo, 'Polish Dance'
1887	September, Glee Club, Miss Weaver, piano solo
1889	February, Gospel Temperance meeting, Miss Weaver and Miss Marcroft, duet
1889	June, Gospel Temperance meeting, Miss Weaver, song, 'Father, don't you hear the angels?'
1889	July, Gospel Temperance meeting, Miss Weaver, song
1889	July, Gospel Temperance meeting, Miss Weaver and Master Ryan, duet
1889	July, Newton Olive Branch Band of Hope, Miss Weaver, song, 'Robin Adair'
1889	November, Gospel Temperance meeting, solo 'very sweetly sung, by Miss Weaver'
1890	August, Newton Olive Branch Band of Hope, Miss Weaver sang 'Sleep, my little blue-eyed treasure' 'very touchingly'
1890	February, concert for the Kingsland Drum and Fife Band, Miss Weaver, song
1890	August, Gospel Temperance meeting, Miss Weaver, solo, 'Have Courage to Say No'
1890	September, Mount Eden Baptist Band of Hope, Miss Weaver, song
1890	September, Star of Newton Lodge, 'Miss Weaver was heard to advantage in her rendition of "The Garden of the Heart".'
1890	September, Star of Newton Lodge, Miss Weaver, song, *'Leave me not in anger, darling'*
1890	October, Eden Terrace Primitive Methodists, Miss Weaver, song, 'There's no one like mother to me'

CHAPTER 8

The Wise Designs of Providence

Map of New Zealand showing where Helen and John lived.

In May 1889, at the age of thirty-one, Elgar married Alice Roberts. Fifteen months later, on 9 August 1890, at the age of twenty-nine, Helen Weaver married twenty-nine-year-old John Munro at St Paul's Anglican Church in Auckland. Built in 1841, St Paul's was the most prominent church in the city, where the military paraded on Sundays and the Masonic fraternity occasionally marched to wearing their full regalia. Together with other heritage buildings, it was demolished in 1885 to pave the way for a restructuring of the Auckland landscape, a move that was afterwards much regretted. A temporary church was built, which lasted for the ten years it took to build the new St Paul's church. No photographs have been found of the temporary church, in which Helen and John were married. The marriage witnesses were Alice Robinson and schoolmaster Henry J.

Carson. Henry Carson had studied at University College London and was already teaching natural science at Auckland College and Grammar School when Helen arrived in New Zealand in 1885. He also taught Latin, English, and maths. Teachers generally taught all subjects, but specialists were called in for natural science (chemistry and physics), French, drawing, and music.

John Munro was born in Glasgow in 1861, and the following year, the family emigrated to New Zealand in the *Lady Egidia*. They landed at Dunedin on the South Island, the city most favoured by the Scots, but soon moved and settled in Invercargill. John's father, also named John, was a bookseller and stationer but realised that there was more money to be made from cattle and, in 1864, took out an auctioneer's licence. Two years later, the family moved to Westport, where John Sen. established himself as a successful merchant and auctioneer. He devoted much time to public affairs and held numerous public offices: he was a member of the Westport Borough Council and served a term as mayor; he was the first secretary of the Westport Hospital Board and was the MP for the Buller district for three years, 1881–4.

At the age of twelve, John Jun. began work in his father's office and gained four years' commercial experience. In December 1877, he went to work in the Bank of New South Wales in Westport and in 1882 was transferred to the Auckland branch as a teller, giving and receiving money and keeping the accounts in large, heavy ledgers. Excellent handwriting was essential, and poor writers were threatened with dismissal. Social and moral impositions meant that officers were not allowed to stay in hotels or inns nor play billiards on public tables. The starting annual salary for a junior was £20, and members of staff were not allowed to marry until they were earning at least £70 per annum, which would be at about the age of thirty. This imposition ensured that bank officers were not reduced to marital poverty.

On 20 August 1890, eleven days after their wedding, John took up the position of manager at the Bank of New South Wales's branch in Patea, three hundred miles away. Helen remained in Auckland for several more weeks, perhaps attending to the removals, as women did. In June 1891, it was Alice who oversaw the Elgars' move from London to Forli, in Malvern Link. In March 1899, while Elgar was on the golf course and taking long walks, it was Alice again who saw to the removals from Forli to Craeglea in Malvern Wells. Helen continued to sing and play for a few weeks after her marriage, but she is not mentioned in Auckland newspapers after October 1890.

Queen Street, Auckland, c.1884 with its banking and commercial premises. The third building down on the right, set back from the road, is the Bank of New South Wales, where John Munro was working when he met Helen. The bank was designed in 1880 by William Armson of Christchurch, with a view to having the 'good effect of removing several one-storey "shanties" which are at present a sad disfigurement to Queen-street, and which have survived the fire epoch.'[36] (Photograph from Alexander Turnbull Library, Wellington, NZ, Ref. No. F-51071-1/2.)

Bank officer John Munro sang and played the organ. He may have met Helen at the bank, at concerts, or at other social events. (Photograph courtesy of Catherine Ives.)

---

[36] T. Hodgson, *The Heart of Colonial Auckland, 1865–1910*, 22.

Egmont Street, Patea, c.1920. Set in the Taranaki District, on the west coast of the North Island, Patea was a small farming community noted only for its port. Cattle and sheep farming was steadily replaced by dairy farming, and in 1894, a dairy factory opened. A freezing centre developed into the town's chief industry. (Photograph from F. G Radcliffe Collection, Alexander Turnbull Library, Wellington, N.Z Ref. No. G-6069-1/2)

The Bank of New South Wales, Patea (from the centennial issue of the *Patea Mail*, 9 September 1981).

The single-storey bank was built in 1875, and in 1881, an additional storey was added to provide residential accommodation. This was Helen and John's home for the next nineteen years. Patea suffered during the depression of the 1880s, '90s, and early 1900s, which may be why the accommodation was not modernised or maintained. In 1901, John wrote an embittered letter to the bank inspector summarising the deficiencies. All the entrances to the house, John pointed out, were deliberately facing the prevailing coastal winds. He said that because there was no bathroom the family had to wash in the kitchen, which was so grim that for the last two and a half years, the family had been forced to eat all their meals at a local hotel. Their live-in servant, he added, would normally have spent her off-duty time in the kitchen, but because it 'was not fit for any human being's leisure time', she used the dining room instead. Each of the four bedrooms was so small that they were only suitable for single occupancy, causing major rearrangements of the household whenever John was away overnight and a bedroom had to be found for the second officer. That had been going on since September 1891, when John had been appointed acting manager of the branch at Waitotara, fourteen miles away. He had to be there every Friday while his two assistants carried on the day-to-day work at the Patea branch. John drew up some plans for alterations, which were carried out a few months later. It was to be many years later, in 1904, that the premises were painted. The local newspaper remarked that, as indicated from the date on the outside of the building (the Bank of New South Wales was founded in 1817), it was probably that long since it was last painted.

Family and Social Life

John had a prestigious position in the community. He joined in events connected with local politics, banking, and religion, and lost no time joining Patea's social life. In September 1890, he sang a duet with Mrs Gush at a fundraising event for the English Church Building Fund. Unfortunately the event was badly attended because of poor advertising and the children's choruses 'were not all that could have been desired'.[37] Shortly after Helen's arrival in Patea, another concert was held to raise money for the same cause. John was enthusiastic but not as polished at music as he was at accountancy. He sang 'The Sentry' from *Iolanthe* 'with good effect', reported the newspaper kindly, 'but to those not conversant with the opera, much of the telling satire in which Mr Gilbert shines was lost'. John also sang another song from *Iolanthe* as part of a trio, which 'showed want of practise, but portions of it were effective and pleasing'. Fortunately, 'Mrs Munro played most of the accompaniments in a finished style'.[38]

Helen and John attended St George's Anglican Church. The church, described as 'an A-frame of five equilateral triangles, two sides of each forming the roof rafters which are carried down to the floor level . . . projecting beyond the walls functioning as buttresses, providing stability

---

[37] *Wanganui Chronicle* (13 September 1890).
[38] *Wanganui Chronicle* (5 January 1891).

in the coastal Patea winds', was consecrated on 5 March 1885.[39] For many years from 1892, John was the church's auditor. He was also auditor of the Men and Boys' Club and the Horse Racing Club and, at one time, President of the Patea Tennis Club, and a member of the Kilwinning Lodge of Freemasons, for whom he played the organ. He was elected to various subcommittees and in 1906 was on the committee of businessmen that discussed the Taranaki exhibit at the Christchurch International Exhibition. When banquets were held to honour notable local men or important men retired or moved away or when a new mayor was installed, John was there to propose toasts on their banking and commercial interests. On such occasions, he mixed with the most important and influential men in the community, notably the vicar, the chairman of Patea County Council, the chairman of the Patea Harbour Board, and the mayor of Patea.

St George's Church, Patea, is listed with the NZ Historic Places Trusts as a Category I significant building. (Photograph from the centennial issue of the *Patea Mail*, 9 September 1981.)

As befitted her social position, Helen did not have paid employment; the 1896 electoral roll records her being engaged in 'domestic duties'. Like Alice Elgar, Helen's role was to maintain the household and support her husband. She was involved in local activities including the annual winter socials, which seemed always to include dancing. Together with several local ladies, Helen helped to organise the Patea Ladies Ball in July 1891, decorating the hall with ferns, palms, and flags. Dancing started at 8.30 and lasted all evening; the ball was said to be 'the most brilliant and successful of any that

---

[39] Quoted from an information board outside the church.

have been held in the district'. The 1893 Bachelors' Ball was well-attended; among those present was Mrs Munro in cream satin. 'The programme was noticeable for the large number of waltzes . . . Dancing was kept up till 5 a.m, and all agreed that the ball was the best ever held in Patea.'[40] The annual winter social in July 1895 comprised a concert followed by a dance. There were eleven items on the concert programme; John sang a solo, 'Thy Foe', and another song in a male quartet. After the concert, the hall was cleared, and everyone danced until midnight.

---

[40] *Wanganui Herald* (22 August 1893).

CHAPTER 9

A Zealous and Energetic Quartet

The parish registers, held at St George's Church, Patea, show that Helen and John had two children in Patea, who both survived to adulthood. Kenneth was born on 7 July 1891 and Joyce on 16 February 1893. They were baptised at St George's Anglican Church on 9 June 1893.

By the time Elgar began to write his 'Enigma Variations', in October 1898, Helen was married to a 'zealous and energetic' bank manager, as he was once described by his staff; she had the prospects of a happy, affluent, respectable, comfortable life with a seven-year-old son and a five-year-old daughter. Their friends included other bank managers and their families.

Kenneth

Helen and John wanted the best education for their children. In 1905, Kenneth was sent as a boarder to the exclusive, fee-paying Nelson Boys' College, which was founded in 1859 on the north-western tip of the South Island. The college's most famous Old Boy was Ernest Rutherford (1871–1937) whose scientific investigations laid the foundation of our understanding of radioactivity.

Nelson College. (Photograph from Alexander Turnbull Library, Wellington, NZ, Ref. No.G-11481-1/1.)

Kenneth was a good all-rounder. He was academic, interested in athletics and drama, and had a jolly sense of humour. At the pre-Christmas prize-giving, in the summer of 1905, he won a prize for the best exam pass in Standard VI. In September 1907, the college dramatic club acted scenes from *King John* and Sheridan's *The Rivals*, in which Kenneth played the part of Bob Acres. He and some other boys also gave demonstrations of club swinging and dumb-bells. That was the year Kenneth became a prefect. In 1909, the drama club put on a variety of acts including the farce *Box and Cox*, in which Kenneth took the part of Mrs Bouncer, the lady of the double-let room. The editorial in the local newspaper pronounced that he 'showed himself an actor of great promise. His enunciation was clear and he acted with freedom and vigour, making the most of the ludicrous opportunities which the play affords'. The second half of the show opened with the stage set as a plantation scene and several boys dressed as 'colored gemmen'. Kenneth was dressed as Uncle Remus and made the most of a humorous monologue. In his final year at the college, 1908–1909, Kenneth was appointed head boy, and at the end-of-summer-term breaking-up ceremony in December 1909, he won the Principal's Prize as Head of House and the Moeller Medal for Head of School. From 1910–2 Kenneth took the law course at Victoria College, Wellington, studying modules in English literature, Latin, jurisprudence, and constitutional history. He took an active part in the social life of the college and was a member of the VUC Tennis Club. He acted in college theatricals and was one of the main participants in the college's 1911 drama extravaganza. At the same time, he completed a year's officer training and reached the rank of second lieutenant. Kenneth was admitted as a solicitor of the Supreme Court, moved to Stratford where he became a law clerk in the office of solicitor William G. Malone, and continued his studies.

Joyce

Joyce was sent to Nelson Girls' College, which opened in 1883. The New Zealand education authorities disapproved of exclusive, fee-paying private schools, so from 1903, if girls passed a proficiency exam, they had two years' free education (known as Removes) paid for by the state. Joyce won a scholarship to Nelson. As well as academic subjects, the girls learned cookery, sewing, dressmaking, elocution, and 'physical culture'. They were encouraged to have an all-round general knowledge and to read books and magazines other than those they encountered at the school and were expected to observe everything around them. Sporty girls could swim, play tennis, hockey, or water polo, and those less physical might join the Christian Union. Joyce was a popular, hard-working girl and did well at school. In 1906 she won a prize for reading; in 1907, a special prize for reading, the prize for the most unselfish boarder, and the British and Foreign Sailors' Society's challenge shield for an essay she wrote on the history of New Zealand as indicated by the use of foreign place names. The following year, she won the Good Fellowship prize and a special prize for reading. At the end of each year, pupils could sit the Civil Service examination; successful pupils under seventeen years old won a free place for two years. Joyce passed in 1908. That was the first year she won the fancy dress prize at the school swimming gala when she dressed up as a clown—and acted the part. In 1909, she won a prize for general excellence. At that year's swimming gala, she dressed up as the Mad Hatter and was so entertaining that she was awarded another prize for the best fancy dress. In 1910, Joyce passed the university matriculation and solicitors' general knowledge.

At the beginning of August 1909, after nineteen years in Patea, John transferred to the bank's branch at Stratford, thirty-six miles from Patea and eight miles from Mount Egmont. The town was originally named Stratford-on-Patea, emulating Stratford-upon-Avon, and the streets were given Shakespearean names.

This photograph of the Munro family was taken in the early 1900s. Catherine and John Munro, in the centre, are surrounded by their children and grandchildren. Helen's husband John is second from the left at the back, and Joyce Munro is the little girl in white seated at the front. Kenneth and Helen are not in this picture. (Photograph courtesy of Catherine Ives.)

Stratford and Hastings

The Bank of New South Wales, Stratford (from *Stratford District Centenary 1878–1978*).

> A large and representative meeting was held at Patea on Wednesday to arrange a public farewell to Mr J. Munro, late manager of the Bank of New South Wales, Patea.' It was decided that a social evening be held on August 10, and that a presentation be made to Mr Munro. A subscription list was opened in the room, and a sum of £30 was guaranteed by those present. Messrs G. V. Pearce, M.P., Christensen (Mayor), McKenna, Horner, Williams, Thompson, Kennedy, Beamish, G. D. Hamerton, and Grainger were appointed a committee with power to add. Mr E. C. Horner was appointed secretary and treasurer. The illuminated address is to bear the signature of those participating.

Helen and John were given a warm farewell when they left Patea, as this newspaper article shows (*Hawera & Normanby Star*, 31 July 1909).

A few days after they left, Helen and John went back to Patea for a euchre party to be held in their honour. Euchre, a four-handed card game, was very popular in New Zealand, America, and Canada. John and Helen had clearly played before. Euchre parties usually ended up with a dance.

Helen and John were in Stratford for almost five years. The 1911 electoral roll records John as bank manager and Helen as married, but little else is known of their lives here except that in 1910, John was admitted to the Council of the New Zealand Society of Accountants. In September 1910, Mrs and Miss Munro qualified for the ladies' Manawatu croquet championships by winning the bogey foursomes '5 down with handicap 18'. These ladies were not mentioned in newspapers before 1910 nor after 1912, so probably they were Helen and Joyce. In March 1911, Mrs and Miss Munro travelled to play in the Hawera versus Stratford croquet

This postcard photograph of Joyce and Kenneth was taken on a holiday to their family at Westport c.1909. (Photograph courtesy of Catherine Ives.)

match, and in January 1912, the Hawera ladies visited Stratford. In her match, Mrs Munro lost, 28–0, and at the return match in March lost both her singles and doubles matches.

The Hawkes Bay earthquake on 3 February 1931 destroyed or made unusable all the banks in Hastings apart from the Bank of New South Wales, which was made of wood. (Photograph from Alexander Turnbull Library, Wellington, NZ, Ref. No. G-2995-1/1.)

In April 1914, John was transferred to Hastings, 140 miles east of Stratford. By the first decade of the twentieth century, it was one of the most thriving towns of the North Island. Apart from the three banks, six hotels, four churches, and numerous public buildings, the town had several industries including a sash and door factory, coach factory, agricultural implement factory, wool-scouring works, brewery, bacon-curing factory, butter factory, and two large freezing works. Set in parkland was the most modern racecourse in the country with an impressive grandstand, beautiful walks, avenues of trees, and an artificial lake overhung with willows. The town claimed to be 'the Leipzig of New Zealand' because of the number of vocal, orchestral, and dramatic societies there. There was an orchestral society, brass band, amateur operatic society, and philharmonic society, but no evidence so far that Helen was involved in any of them.

John was replaced at the Stratford branch by his friend Walter Leversedge, and two years later, in August 1916, Walter's son, Graham, was born in Stratford; Joyce was his godmother. When asked about Joyce and Helen, Graham said that all his family possessions were destroyed in the 1931 Napier earthquake, so he had to rely on 'a somewhat faulty memory'. He said that all he remembered of his godmother was that she lived in

Taranaki; that she had left him £50 in her will, and that she had given him 'a beautiful model, quite a large one, of Sir Thomas Lipton's yacht, *Rainbow*, the challenger for the America's Cup'. The Leversedges moved to Napier in September 1923, and Graham remembered his godmother coming to the bank of New South Wales at Napier and giving him the yacht, but he recalled that she was a young woman. The lady could not have been Joyce, who died in 1921; it must have been Helen.

CHAPTER 10

The Thirteenth Enigma?

This chapter addresses the possible identity of Enigma Variation XIII, which was entitled *Romanza* and inscribed ***. For over half a century, two candidates have been seriously tipped to be the recipients of this honour: Lady Mary Lygon, who was a friend of the Elgars at the time the Variations were written, and Elgar's former fiancée, Helen Weaver.

Elgar Alone

On 20 July 1884, Elgar replied to his invitation to Dr Buck's wedding:

> I will not worry you with particulars but must tell you that things have not prospered with me this year at all, my prospects are worse than ever & to crown my miseries my engagement is broken off and I am lonely. Perhaps at some future time I may come out of my shell again but at present I remain here; I have not the heart to speak to anyone. Please give my kind regards to Mrs. Buck & all friends; & once more accept my good wishes for your happiness, these I can give you the more sincerely since I know what it is to have lost my own forever.[41]

The shock and misery of his broken engagement affected Elgar's health, and on 4 August 1884, he went on a solo tour of Scotland to recover, to take his mind off the events of the past few weeks, and to get away from Worcester, the unhappy stage of those events. He later explained to Buck his reasons for going. 'About my Scots excursion—I got into a very desponding state (you ken what happened) and it behoved me to do something out of the common to raise my spirits . . .'[42] When he returned to Worcester, Elgar started some new compositions but admitted to Charles Buck in a letter dated 8 March that 'of course all these things are of no account—but they

---

[41] Quoted in Northrop Moore, *A Creative Life*, 104.
[42] Northrop Moore, *A Creative Life*, 106.

serve to divert me & hide a broken heart.'[43] Supposing that the engagement to Helen had ended in January 1884, then Elgar was still suffering miserably fourteen months later.

On 10 August 1885, Elgar set to music an 1870 poem, *Through the Long Days* by statesman and poet John Milton Hay (1838–1905). Hay was a former private secretary and assistant to Abraham Lincoln and later served as the United States secretary of state. His words capture how Elgar felt about Helen. Selecting a poem containing the phrase 'while my darling lives' may indicate that Elgar had already heard a rumour that Helen had a potentially fatal lung complaint.

>Through the long days and years
>What will my loved one be,
>Parted from me?
>Through the long days and years.
>
>Always as then she was
>Loveliest, brightest, best,
>Blessing and blest,
>Always as then she was.
>
>Never on earth again
>Shall I before her stand,
>Touch lip or hand,
>Never on earth again.
>
>But while my darling lives
>Peaceful I journey on,
>Not quite alone,
>Not while my darling lives.

By July 1886, a full two years after the engagement ended, the dismal tide had turned. Elgar wrote to Buck, 'I have been coming out of my shell lately; went to a large picnic with sister Lucy last week; high jinks; . . . I helped to boil the kettle &c &c flirting (out of practice), dancing (stiff in the joints) . . .'[44] and added that he was playing tennis again. Then a flood of

---

[43] Northrop Moore, 111.
[44] Northrop Moore, 114.

good fortune began. Elgar made a teaching appointment in his diary for 6 October with a new pupil, 'Miss Roberts 1st lesson'.

A Portrait of Lady Mary Lygon

Lady Mary Lygon, c. 1895.

Lady Mary Lygon (1869–1927), the daughter of Frederick, Sixth Earl Beauchamp, was born on 26 February 1869. When her father died unexpectedly, Lady Mary's elder brother William (1872–1938), then only nineteen years old, took the title Seventh Earl Beauchamp. Educated at Eton and Oxford, he held several government posts including privy counsellor, Lord Steward of the Household, and Lord Warden of the Cinque Ports. He was the only cabinet minister available, on 4 August 1914, to witness the signing of the declaration of war by the king. A colourful character, Beauchamp was depicted as Lord Marchmain in Evelyn Waugh's *Brideshead Revisited*. After his homosexuality was discovered, he sought voluntary exile abroad and died in 1938 at New York's Waldorf Astoria. He was buried at Madresfield.

William did not marry until 1902, so Lady Mary acted as mayoress when he was mayor of Worcester, 1895–6, and accompanied him to Australia where she presided over Government House when he took up his position as governor of New South Wales, 1899–1902. When she was away from the family home, Madresfield Court near Malvern in Worcestershire, Lady Mary moved in royal circles. In 1897 she was appointed lady-in-waiting to the Duchess of York at St James's Palace, and she accompanied the duchess and her husband on a tour of the colonies. In 1901 she was appointed woman of the bedchamber to the Princess of Wales and in 1904 as her lady-in-waiting. Lady Mary attended many royal functions during the reign of Edward VII and in 1910 was appointed lady-in-waiting to Queen Mary.

When she was at Madresfield, Lady Mary arranged concerts and musical competitions in and around Malvern. She was also much interested in the musical education of local schoolchildren, arranging inter-school competitions and talks such as 'Sight Reading in Schools'. From the late 1890s, she wrote frequently to Elgar, perhaps asking him to play at one of her concerts, to judge a competition, or just to give her his news. In a letter of 4 April 1898 to 'Mr Elgar', Lady Mary hoped he would be available to discuss the forthcoming musical competition with him, adding that if they met at Madresfield she could show him and Mrs Elgar her garden, which was looking rather nice. She signed the letter 'Yours sincerely, Mary Lygon'. Her letters to the Elgars were always chatty and friendly, but by the early 1900s she ended them 'Yours affectionately', a term used between intimate friends. In a letter to the Elgars dated 4 June 1902, she told them how delighted the family was at Beauchamp's engagement. By referring to her brother by his title, Beauchamp, Lady Mary regarded the Elgars as social equals. Lady Mary occasionally spent whole days with the Elgars, either at her home or theirs. She was a friend of both Edward and Alice Elgar, and their friendship continued until the 1920s. There is no evidence that Elgar was attracted to Lady Mary in an intimate or romantic way.

Lady Mary Lygon's family home was here at Madresfield Court, on the outskirts of Malvern.

In May 1905, at the age of thirty-six, Lady Mary married Major the Hon. Henry Forbes Trefusis at a quiet family service in Madresfield Church. Among the wedding gifts was a silver string box from Sir Edward and Lady Elgar.

The Possible Identity of Enigma Variation XIII

Below is a list of ten unequivocal facts about Enigma XIII:

1. Basil Nevinson was once considered as the subject (Elgar's early draft).
2. Enigma XIII was dedicated to a lady (Elgar's own words).

3. On an early sketch sheet of the Variations, Elgar wrote 'LML' against Enigma XIII
4. Lady Mary's initials do not appear on the finished version.
5. Three asterisks replaced the initials LML.
6. A quotation was incorporated from Mendelssohn's 'Calm Sea and Prosperous Voyage' overture.
7. The subject was at sea at the time of composition (Elgar's own words).
8. Lady Mary was not at sea at the time of composition.
9. Enigma XIII was not inscribed 'Romanza' while Nevinson and Lady Mary were being considered.
10. Enigma XIII became a romanza.

Below are thirteen considerations for speculation and interpretation:

1. Elgar initially included Lady Mary in his list of Variations, and she concurred, but she said he could not use her initials for a romanza. Jerrold Northrop Moore observed that 'the character of this music with her name attached would be certain to set local tongues wagging'.[45] Lady Mary and Elgar were born into, and lived in, different social circles. In the twenty-first century, it is almost impossible to understand the social chasm there once was between a tradesman's son and a member of the English aristocracy. Rosa Burley wrote as recently as 1948, 'Today, when social distinctions seem to be fading from existence, it is hard to understand the rigidity with which they were maintained during the reign of Queen Victoria.'[46] Thus a romance between Elgar and Lady Mary would have offended the conventions of the period in which they lived; a romanza could not be privately or publicly dedicated to her. Elgar would not wish to embarrass Lady Mary, Alice, or himself so dedicated the piece to someone else.
2. Elgar dedicated Enigma XIII to Lady Mary as he had planned and, for reasons that no one knows, changed her initials to asterisks.
3. Elgar identified Lady Mary as a potential Variation, but when he asked her permission, even before the piece was finished, she told him she did not wish to be a Variation even if it were anonymous.
4. Lady Mary knew nothing about the proposed dedication; Elgar never told her.

---

[45] Northrop Moore, *Spirit of England*, 35.
[46] R. Burley and F. Carruthers, *Edward Elgar: The Record of a Friendship*, 44.

5. During the course of composing Op. 36, Elgar changed his mind several times; he changed his mind about the friends to be included and their position in the Enigma numbering. Nicholas Kilburn and Ivor Atkins, once both contenders as Friends, were eventually rejected. Renumbering included Nimrod, who moved from XI to IX; Dorabella from XII to X; Troyte from IX to VII; Ysobel from IV to VI. Elgar did consider Lady Mary as Enigma XIII when he began the work, as he had done with Nevinson, but perhaps he changed his mind. He wrote a romanza and exchanged LML for ***; these three asterisks may have represented LML or someone else.

6. a) The 'Calm Sea and Prosperous Voyage' passage was not written with Lady Mary Lygon in mind because she was not at sea in 1898.

   b) The 'Calm Sea and Prosperous Voyage' passage was written with Lady Mary Lygon in mind, but later, Elgar forgot that she had not been at sea at the time of composition. There is no evidence that Helen Weaver was at sea in 1898 and, if she were, no reason to think Elgar knew of it.

7. Writers on the subject have had their uncertainties. Percy Young in 1955 noted that 'some doubts have, from time to time, been expressed regarding the "portraiture" of Lady Mary Lygon . . .'[47] Rosa Burley, who was associated with Elgar for many years, wrote that 'Edward told me quite clearly and unequivocally whom it represented and I always supposed that his reason for withholding this lady's name was that extremely intimate and personal feelings were concerned'. She added that 'the throbbing and the quotation from "Calm Sea and Prosperous Voyage" . . . bore no reference to the liner and the sea voyage which were afterwards associated with this variation but, as might be expected in a movement named "Romanza", expressed something very different.'[48] This suggests that the sea voyage was a red herring. Burley did not intimate the Variation's identity.

8. Ernest Newman's choice was Helen Weaver. Late in life, Elgar had confided to Newman his past attachment to Helen. In the *Sunday Times* in November 1956, Newman wrote that the music of Variation XIII was too deeply emotional to be associated with the platonic relationship Elgar had with Lady Mary Lygon. 'There is much expression of personal experiences in this music . . . It is time we heard the last of the old legend that the subject of this variation was Lady Mary Lygon . . . A

---

[47] P. Young, *Elgar O. M.* (1955), 281.
[48] R. Burley and F. Carruthers, *Edward Elgar: The Record of a Friendship*, 125.

present-day listener must be devoid of sensibility if he does not see that, whoever the human subject of the No 13 may have been, it is a poignant brooding upon some personal experience or other that made a profound and enduring mark on him . . . That moving sound picture of the throbbing of the engines of a great liner and the sad quotation from Mendelssohn's "Calm Sea and Prosperous Voyage" overture would never have been wrung out of Elgar by the fact that the good lady at Madresfield . . . had chosen to go on a sea trip. A study merely off Elgar's scoring of the variation should make it clear to any person of more than average sensitivity that he was here dwelling in imagination on somebody and something the parting from whom and which had at some time or other torn the very heart out of him.'[49]Newman suggested that the Variation concerned the parting with the Leipzig girl.

9. In May 1939, Newman told Alice Stuart Wortley's daughter, Clare, that he had been told by a mutual friend of Elgar's the identity of the subject of the asterisks. The friend had confirmed that the subject was not Lady Mary Lygon.

10. Elgar's sisters, Lucy and Polly, were godparents to Frank Weaver's children, and Weaver family descendants believe that in the 1890s, Elgar was giving Frank's sons violin lessons. A chance remark in Elgar's presence by any one of those people in the autumn of 1898 may have triggered a memory of Helen.

11. Late in life, Elgar disclosed his feelings about Helen to Ivor Atkins, so Atkins's choice that Variation XIII be played at Elgar's memorial service in March 1934 may be significant. This is a valid consideration though does not prove that Helen Weaver and *** were synonymous.

12. The assumption has always been that Opus 36, Variations on an Original Theme was written wholly in 1898. Julian Rushton, whose unequivocal choice is Lady Mary, observed that Opus 36 was completed notably quickly, 'if he [Elgar] had no intimation of the work before 21 October 1898'.[50] The speed of composition may be explained if Elgar had already written one or more parts some years earlier. In a letter of 7 October 1885, Elgar informed Charles Buck that Helen, suffering from a lung affliction, was leaving for New Zealand later that month. Perhaps, broken-hearted and fearing her imminent death, he began to write some music that same month, resurrecting it in another October thirteen

---

[49] *The Sunday Times* (25 November 1956). The newspaper's music critic, Hugh Mortimer Cecil (1868–1959), used the pseudonym Ernest Newman.

[50] J. Rushton, *Elgar: 'Enigma' Variations,* 15.

years later. He added the 'Calm Sea and Prosperous Voyage' theme, knowing retrospectively that it was true, and hid Helen's identity by the use of three asterisks. That would also explain the veracity of Elgar's own words, 'The asterisks take the place of the name of a lady who was, at the time of composition, on a sea voyage.'[51]

13. When Elgar inscribed Enigma XIII 'LML' he could not have foreseen the interest of future generations in that attribute. If the draft bearing those initials had been destroyed, no one would have known that he was even considering Lady Mary. If that draft had not survived, who might we nominate as the subject of XIII?

---

[51] E. Elgar, *My Friends Pictured Within*

CHAPTER 11

'Flotsam on the Fringe of Hell'

(M. E. Hankins's description of soldiers in *Chronicles of the NZEF*)

At the outbreak of war, Kenneth was living and working in Stratford. He was disappointed at not being selected to join the main expeditionary force, unlike his employer, fifty-six-year-old William G. Malone. On 3 September, Kenneth wrote to a Nelson Old Boy, Colonel Chaytor, about his suitability for call-up. He mentioned that in his fifth and final year at the school, 1909, he had been the school captain. He had also been the senior subaltern of Nelson College Rifle Cadet Corps and had passed the examination for lieutenant. He added that from 1910–11 he had completed a year's service in the Victoria College Officers' Training Corps, a year in the Victoria College Rifles 1911–12 and two years as an officer in the Eleventh Regiment Taranaki Rifles. All he wanted, he said, was 'to uphold the military traditions of Nelson College' and to be selected if any reinforcements were sent.

Kenneth was a member of the Territorial Force with the Taranaki (Rifles) Regiment. His war record shows that he was 5 feet 6½ inches tall, weighed 187 lbs, and was of fair complexion with fair hair and blue eyes. His creed was Unitarian.

Despite early enlistment preventing him from completing his law degree, on 31 December 1914 Kenneth joined the Wellington Infantry Regiment as second lieutenant. He was promoted to first lieutenant in February 1915, and on 17 April he embarked with the Fourth Reinforcements on HMNZ troop ship SS *Knight Templar*. Kenneth was just one of one hundred thousand men in the Australian and New Zealand Army Corps (ANZAC) who sailed to Europe and North Africa in 1914–18. He arrived at Suez on 26 May 1915 and headed for Gallipoli. The allied forces first landed in Gallipoli on 25 April 1915, and that

78

day has remained a poignant reminder of the brave men who died in defence of their motherland. Every year ANZAC Day, 25 April, is a public holiday enabling everyone in New Zealand to pay their respects to the fallen.

Kenneth's commanding officer was his employer, Lt Col. Malone. Malone had fought in the Franco–Prussian War, was in command of the Eleventh Taranaki Rifles, and commanded the Wellington Infantry Regiment. He wrote from the Dardanelles in 1915, 'I love these men of mine—heroes all, as brave as brave can be. I am under censor rule but I must tell you that the Wellington Infantry Regiment has turned out all that one could wish. The men are splendid and as brave as they make 'em, being cool and enduring. There are no better soldiers in the world. I cannot tell you all of the great work they have done, and I cannot tell you of the losses. The hardships are really solid. The men have been fighting night and day since April 27 up till midnight of the 12th inst.' [52]

Malone was mortally wounded at Sari Bair on 8 August 1915, one of 8,500 ANZACs killed in Gallipoli; a further 25,000 were wounded. He and three of his sons, aged twenty-one, twenty-three, and twenty-five, had all joined the Taranaki section of the expeditionary force. At the time of his death, one son, Terence, had been wounded in the Dardanelles. Edmund was still serving there. Brian, who had been serving in Samoa, hoped to embark soon with the Reinforcements, and Maurice was about to embark with the Sixth Reinforcements. A daughter, Nora, was nursing with the Red Cross in England, and Malone's wife was living in Reading, Berkshire. The entire Malone family had left Stratford. Reports of casualties continued, and Patea's local newspaper reported that 'Lieutenant K. Munro, son of Mr. J. Munro, for many years manager of the Bank of New South Wales at Patea, has been admitted to the Royal Free Hospital, London, where he is making good progress towards recovery from wounds received at the Dardanelles.'[53] On 17 August 1915, Kenneth had been admitted to the sixteenth casualty clearing station but suffering from debility probably caused by enteric fever (typhoid). He embarked for England the same day on the hospital ship *Andania*. By the time he was admitted to the Royal Free Hospital on 31 August, he was also suffering from influenza. On 24 January 1916, after nearly five months in hospital, Kenneth was sent to Grey Towers, a nineteenth-century crenellated mansion in Hornchurch, Essex, (demolished 1931) that had recently been established as a depot for the many sick or wounded New Zealanders arriving in England.

---

[52] *Otago Daily Times* (13 August 1915).
[53] *Hawera & Normanby Star* (5 October 1915).

Grey Towers had its own enteric hospital. (Photograph from Hornchurch During the Great War [1920].)

Grey Towers under snow.

It was hoped to get the men fit enough to send back to the front line in France. If their convalescence were to exceed six months, it was more economical to send them back to New Zealand as the voyage was usually more beneficial than a long stay in hospital away from home. When the men had fully recovered, they rejoined their units in France. On 17 February, Kenneth was again struck off strength on account of ill health. Meanwhile, entertainment was laid on, and at a concert at the camp on 22 March 1916, the New Zealand soprano Rosina Buckman (1881–1948) was one of the performers. It was Rosina Buckman who, in Birmingham on 4 October 1917, sang the first performance of Elgar's setting of Laurence Binyon's poem 'The Fourth of August'.

Edward Elgar, Kenneth Munro, and Frank Weaver

Brian Trowell, a former professor of music at Oxford, believes that Elgar discovered that Kenneth was in England. It was well known that there were New Zealand soldiers in London because of the publicity accorded to a memorial service in Westminster Abbey on 26 April 1916 commemorating the soldiers who had died at Gallipoli. The service was attended by New Zealander Lt A. E. Alexander, who may have been the musician A. Alexander, whom Alice recorded in her diary in September 1916 as going to tea, and to whom Elgar was very kind. Alexander visited them again in October. One Elgar diary entry suggests that Alexander was supporting Clara Butt, who was the first to sing 'To Women' and 'For the Fallen' which, together with 'The Fourth of August', comprised Elgar's *The Spirit of England*. It is unlikely that Alexander knew of any connection between New Zealander Lt Kenneth Munro and Englishman Sir Edward Elgar. Elgar's sisters Lucy and Polly, as godmothers to Frank Weaver's children, may have passed on word of Helen and her family to their brother. However, Frank's daughter Maria Theresa said she always regretted not finding out about 'Aunt Nelly', suggesting that Helen was rarely, if ever, mentioned.

Might Frank Weaver himself have conveyed news of Kenneth to Elgar? Frank and Elgar were friends for perhaps twenty years or more. They came from similar backgrounds, had shared interests, and were both very close to Helen, but their later lives polarised. After his father's death in 1880, Frank took over the boot and shoe business at 84 High Street. In August 1887, at the age of thirty-two, he married Fannie Jones at Upton Warren church. One of the witnesses was Bob Surman who, for many years, had played in orchestras with Frank and Elgar. Frank had played the double bass and Elgar the trombone, and as a wedding gift, Elgar composed for his old friend a duet for trombone and double bass. An allegretto of forty-nine bars, it is in the form of a fugue in which the subject is first played by the double bass, then echoed by the trombone. Elgar presented the piece to Frank on 1 August 1887. The manuscript was inherited by one of Frank's sons and eventually published in 1970 by Rodney Slatford, a double bass player and founder of the Nash Ensemble. The remainder of Frank's life was pieced together in the early 1980s with the help of Maria Theresa, her daughter Jane, and Sr Eanswythe Edwards, OSB, of Stanbrook Abbey, Callow End, Worcester.

Frank's first child, Marguerite, was born in November 1888 and baptised at Claines Church, where her grandfather had married as a boy, nearly fifty years earlier. By the age of twelve, Marguerite was attending a Roman Catholic convent boarding school in Loughborough. She was destined to become a brilliant musician, known as the English Nightingale, but tragically died in 1914 and was buried in Vienna.

On 2 May 1889, six days before his marriage, Elgar wrote in his diary 'presentd. with Dressing Bag Messrs Wall. & Weaver', confirming that he was still in touch with Frank. In the 1890s, Frank lived here at Severn Lodge, Stephenson Terrace; Elgar was living in Malvern Link, just a few miles away. The Elgar diaries do not record that the two men ever met and, if there was correspondence, none survives. It is said in the Weaver family that Elgar gave Frank's sons violin lessons. Elgar gave up teaching around August 1899 when the boys were eight and five years old respectively, so they would have been quite young when—or if— he gave them lessons.

Frank and Fannie moved to Severn Lodge, Stephenson Terrace, a large, elegant villa overlooking Worcester racecourse. Their first son, Francis [Frank] Schubert, was born there in July 1891 and baptised at Upton Warren. On 25 May 1901, when he was still a lad, Francis was rebaptised at St George's Roman Catholic Church, where Elgar had been baptised years earlier. As a young man, Francis trained for the priesthood at a Roman Catholic seminary in London, and was ordained subdeacon in September 1923. In February 1930, he made his solemn profession in St Peter's church at Stonyhurst Jesuit College in Lancashire. Francis's brother, John Bernard (Jack) was born at Severn Lodge in February 1894. He was baptised at St George's the same day that his elder brother was rechristened;

Elgar's sister Polly (Mary Susannah Grafton) was godmother to them both. Jack trained as an altar boy at Stanbrook Abbey, attended a Roman Catholic college at Eckington in Derbyshire, and in July 1926 was ordained a Roman Catholic priest at St Bueno's, now a Christian hospitality retreat in North Wales.

The Benedictine abbey of Stanbrook was established in 1838 when a group of nuns moved into Stanbrook Hall at Powick, near Worcester. Stanbrook became world famous for its translation and printing of ancient manuscripts. Fannie Weaver received religious instruction there and in July 1901 was baptised at St George's. In December that year, she made the first of many further visits to Stanbrook Abbey, the first time on her own but afterwards accompanied by her little boys or Marguerite, and sometimes by friends. On 2 September 1902, Frank and Fanny's youngest child, Maria Theresa, was born and baptised at St George's five days later. One of her two godmothers was Elgar's sister Lucy (Pipe). Maria Theresa attended a private school in Worcester, perhaps the convent school run by the Misses Grafton, who were related by marriage to the Elgars. In 1906, when she was only four and a half years old, Maria went to live in the abbey lodge at Stanbrook with her mother and two brothers, and remembers seeing her father only once.

Frank is mentioned in a Worcester trades' directory for 1906 but not in 1910, suggesting that it was between those dates that he abandoned his family and moved to Bournemouth where he took up a semi-vagrant existence as a jobbing musician. It seems that he had always wanted to be a musician; he never wanted to take over the shop and was glad to be rid of it. During the Edwardian era, Bournemouth was expanding fast; there was an active musical life, and it was well-known for its healthy air. Despite the break-up of the family, Frank's two sons kept in touch with both parents, seeing their father in Bournemouth and visiting their mother in Worcester and making visits with her to Stanbrook until 1937. Frank left behind his family, his business, and his income; old-age pensions for the over-seventies had yet to be introduced. Nothing suggests that he ever composed or conducted after leaving Worcester, but slipped quietly into obscurity. He died in Bournemouth in June 1932 aged seventy-six. It is unlikely that Frank ever knew that his nephew, Kenneth, was in England and just as unlikely that Elgar ever knew it.

Three or four years before his death, Frank was instructed in the Roman Catholic faith by Fr James Percival Triggs (1869–1936) of the Sacred Heart Church, Bournemouth, and received into the Roman Catholic Church. The Register of Electors for 1932, the year that Frank died, shows that his son, Fr Francis Weaver, SJ, was living at the Presbytery at the Church of the Sacred Heart.

Frank was buried in Bournemouth's Wimborne Road cemetery, plot T6/21S, which is under the roots of this tree.

Fr Francis died in May 1957 and was buried in East Cemetery, Boscombe, plot W3/226, a grave he shares with three other members of the Society of Jesuits.

Kenneth did not see the Zeppelins flying over Grey Towers on six successive nights at the beginning of June 1916 because he had marched out for France on 14 April. In April 1916, after the Gallipoli campaign and a short stay in Egypt, the New Zealand Division landed in France. It was concentrated near Hazebrouk, approximately 30 km west of Armentières, and it was there that Kenneth was reunited with his regiment. On 16 June, he made his will, in which he left half of the pay he was owed to Miss Alice Macdonald of 212 The Terrace, Wellington, and the other half to his mother in Hastings. His life policy paid £210 8s 4d, and his pay owing was about £20. On 3 July the men from the Second New Zealand Infantry Brigade stormed an enemy trench to kill and capture German soldiers. There were no Germans in the trench, but nevertheless Kenneth was killed by shrapnel during the raid. At home, people learned that 'Lieut. K. Munro, reported killed in action, was the son of Mr. J. Munro, who was for some years the manager of the Bank of New South Wales at Stratford, and now stationed at Hastings. The late Lieut. Munro was on the staff of the late Lieut. Colonel Malone of this town, and was a most enthusiastic and popular volunteer. Very deep regret will be felt on all sides that he has fallen in his country's service.'[54]

LIEUTENANT KENNETH MUNRO,
of Hastings,
Killed in action.

Lieutenant Kenneth Munro (service no. 10/1930) was awarded the 1914–15 Star, the British War Medal, and the Victory Medal.

---

[54] *Hawera & Normanby Star* (29 August 1916).

Fifty other men were killed the same day as Kenneth, either in action or of wounds received. They are buried together in the Cité Bonjean Military Cemetery, Armentières, now an industrial town on the Belgian border, nine miles north-west of Lille. The cemetery was established in October 1914 for military and civilian use, though the civilians were later removed.

Kenneth's death is recorded in the Roll of Honour on the walls of the National War Memorial in Auckland.

On Easter Sunday 2013, the small palm cross on the left of the grave was removed by the author from St George's Church, Patea, where Kenneth was baptised, and placed on his grave in September 2013. The Commonwealth War Grave (CWG) poppy was placed here at the same time.

CHAPTER 12

Finale

In July 1917, John was transferred to Palmerston North, one hundred miles south-west of Hastings. When Joyce had started to show symptoms of the same wasting disease that had killed Helen's stepmother in 1883, she and Helen moved nearly three hundred miles north to Mount Eden, a leafy, lofty suburb of Auckland where the climate was more beneficial to Joyce's health and the medical treatment superior to that further south. They took a house at 2 Kingsview Road.

2 Kingsview Road, Auckland, was built of wood with a corrugated iron roof, c.1914–18. These materials made it cheap to build and able withstand moderate earth tremors. The exterior is more or less how it was originally; inside are original doors, finger plates, ceilings, and stained-glass windows.

Two years later they moved to 26 Pencarrow Road, and it was there, on 6 October 1921, that Joyce died of pulmonary tuberculosis. She was buried two days later in the new family grave in Purewa Cemetery. Consumption was still killing thousands of people annually. In England the figures were high but falling: 1866–70, 2,448; 1871–5, 2,218; 1876–80, 2,040; 1881–5, 1830; 1886–90, 1635; 1891–5, 1462; 1896–90, 1323, and a Royal Commission was under way to investigate a link between bovine and human tuberculosis. For the first quarter of the twentieth century, scientists round the world were trying to identify the causes and treatment of TB.[55]

---

[55] Details from the *Otago Daily Times* (25 February 1908).

26 Pencarrow Road in 1986. It was demolished sometime between 1985 and 2000, and two new town houses were built on the plot.

In February 1922, John retired to Auckland. He and Helen moved to 28 Lucerne Road, Remuera (pronounced rem-you-air-are), a suburb described by Aucklander Noeleen Sutton as a rather 'toney' (upper-class) area. It may have been the collective strain of his demanding job, the years of separation from his wife, and the death of his two children that was responsible for the gastric ulcer that eventually perforated. John died in Auckland hospital on 14 September 1925, aged sixty-four. In his will, which he made in July 1892 when Helen was two months pregnant with Joyce, John left everything to Helen. She continued to live at the house in Lucerne Road.

28 Lucerne Road in 1986. The old tree on the right of the picture is a Poutakawa tree, also known as a New Zealand Christmas tree because it bursts into bright red flowers for about two weeks at Christmas before dying back. It would have flowered at the time Helen died.

28 Lucerne Road was named Elgar House in the 1990s.

By June 1927, Helen knew that she had a cancerous tumour of the intestine. It would have been a painful and undignified end to her life. For six months before her death, she was cared for at the Mater Misericordiae Hospital in Mount Eden. In 1868, Thomas McFarlane built a three-story hillside mansion in Mountain Road. In 1900 the house was taken over by the Sisters of Mercy, who transformed it into the Mater Misericordiae (Mother of Mercy) Hospital. The sisters were Roman Catholic nuns whose duty was to relieve suffering and care for the sick, regardless of gender or religion. Sometimes they visited people at home; at other times, they cared for the sick in the hospital. It was a charitable institution; wealthy patients paid for treatment and the poor were treated free of charge. Before the First World War, isolation huts were built for people suffering from infectious diseases, one of which was TB. In 1918, a new up-to-date surgical unit, Stella Maris, was built, and by the 1920s, Mater Misericordiae was the leading private surgical hospital in Auckland.

Mater Misericordiae Hospital. The picture shows the sister, staff, and visitors at the main entrance at its opening in 1900. The isolation huts and the mansion were demolished in 1981, and the hospital was renamed the Mercy Hospital in 1988. (Photograph courtesy of the Mercy Hospital.)

Helen died at the hospital on 23 December 1927. She was cremated at Waikumete (why-koo-mit-ee) cemetery, and her ashes interred in the family grave (Block A Row 29 Plot 038) at Purewa Cemetery on 9 January 1928. Joyce, John, and Kenneth are mentioned on the gravestone; no one added Helen's name.

Helen's will, which she made on 12 September 1927, tells a little more about her possessions and interests and one sadly significant point: the huge loss of young New Zealander lives in the Great War. One of her two executors was dentist Leonard Horrocks, who lived in Lucerne Road. One of his brothers-in-law, Reg Quilliam, was a law student at Nelson with Kenneth. Reg was killed in France in August 1916. His brother, Lt Cecil Quilliam, was also killed in action in November 1918, at the very end of the conflict. Helen left Leonard her reading desk and £50. She left his wife, Vita, her screenwriting desk—possibly the 'screen and desk in one' that she had inherited from her stepmother in Worcester many years earlier. She also left £50 to Grace Harper, the wife of James Harper, secretary of the Returned Soldiers Pension Board in Wellington. To the scriptorium at Nelson College, Helen bequeathed all her books, 'in memory of my son', directing that any unsuitable books should be sold and the proceeds used to buy something more appropriate. Her records and gramophone were left to Bertha Sinclair, who was the same age as Kenneth. Bertha was a musician, studied at Victoria College at the same time as Kenneth, and qualified as a teacher in 1914. To Brenda Koch, Helen left books and sheet music. Brenda had passed various music exams at school in 1908 and 1909, then went on to Hill Street Convent where, in 1917, she was awarded an advanced grade pass in the Associated Board of the Royal Academy and the Royal College of Music exams. The watercolour of the gypsy encampment by William Clark Eddington that Helen inherited from her stepmother she left to her neighbour Ada Wake, and some silver tableware to Lily Anderson of Mount Eden.

Helen's other executor was a widow, Dagmar Medhurst. Dagmar (née Gilfillan) was born in December 1885; her father, Harry, may have been a business colleague of John's dating back to their days in Patea. Helen left her £50 and a carved chest with a mirror. She also left £50 to Graham Leversedge, 'my late daughter's godson'. Like Elgar, Helen loved animals and left £50 to the Auckland Society for the Prevention of Cruelty to Animals. The remainder of her estate was to be sold, the money invested, and the income paid jointly to John's two spinster sisters, Jessie and Marion Munro. After their deaths, the capital was to be equally divided between the various orphanages in and around Auckland. No Weaver family members were mentioned in her will.

Coda

This book has examined the lives of three people who affected Elgar's life; it has revealed their triumphs and trials, successes and sadness. Annie Groveham met Elgar briefly when she was a young woman. Their paths diverged, and Annie had a brief musical career; she was drawn to the stage and married comfortably. Although the Great War deprived her of her son and her husband, she seems to have lived happily ever after. However, as an older woman past her prime, she renewed her acquaintance with Elgar, perhaps in a nostalgic return to her unadulterated youth.

Napier Roberts was born into class, status, and apparent wealth. With his upper-class background, it is doubtful that his Roman Catholic marriage caused any social ripples, but it set a precedent for his sister to follow suit. Napier was doubtless dignified but distraught with the disgrace of bankruptcy. His financial situation, separation from his wife, and an old age with limited resources doubtless affected his sister, so almost certainly his brother-in-law. Napier's personality and poverty might be summarised thus: 'Folly often drags people out of their happy state and casts them into the utmost misery . . . We can see by a multitude of examples how true it is that folly leads some people from prosperity to disaster.'[56]

Helen Weaver loved Elgar despite his lack of money and success, and it was through their brief but loving courtship that he perhaps learned that love can be lost through lack of money, thus that money can buy love. The most notable differences between Helen Weaver and Alice Roberts were age, class, and wealth, yet they shared common qualities. They were well-educated and proficient pianists with the confidence to perform in public. When they were thrown on the world after their mothers' deaths, they took control of their lives with bold, almost irreversible decisions for the 1880s: marriage and emigration respectively. They were feminine but not feminist, marrying and committing their lives to supporting and successfully enhancing the lives of their husbands and children.

Helen would have returned Elgar's letters to him before re-establishing her life on the other side of the world. She married comfortably and enjoyed the social prestige of a bank manager's wife, but she also suffered the premature deaths of her two children. She must surely have heard about Elgar's triumphant musical career, but did she ever wonder, as we do today, which of Elgar's friends was enshrined in Enigma XIII? Elgar was a seventy-year-old widower when Helen died, and he almost certainly never knew of her death. She would have remained in his mind as she had been when he last saw her—young, beautiful, blue-eyed, and blonde. It is not unreasonable that shortly before he died, he did not look nostalgically back over his life and review the loss of Helen with tender and mixed emotions. But he must have known that had he married her, he would never have achieved the hope and glory of which he was capable. She must have known the same.

---

[56] G. Boccaccio, 'The First Day, Third Story', *Decameron*.

BIBLIOGRAPHY

ALLEN, K., *Gracious Ladies: The Norbury Family and Edward Elgar* (Kevin Allen, 2013).

ATKINS, E. WULSTAN, *The Elgar-Atkins Friendship* (David & Charles, 1984).

BELGRAVE, MICHAEL, *The Mater: A History of Auckland's Mercy Hospital, 1900–2000* (Mercy Hospital, 2000).

BLUNT, WILFRID, *On Wings of Song: A Biography of Felix Mendelssohn* (Hamilton, 1974).

BURLEY, ROSA AND CARRUTHERS, FRANK C., *The Record of a Friendship* Barrie & Jenkins, 1972).

CANNON, RICHARD, *Historical Record of the King's Liverpool Regiment of Foot* (2nd edn, Harrison & Sons, 1883).

CHADWICK, OWEN, *The Victorian Church, Part II* (2nd edn, Adam & Charles Black, 1972).

Cyclopoedia of New Zealand, The (1905, 1908)

DRYSDALE, JOHN, 'A Matter of Wills', in *Elgar's Earnings* (Boydell Press, 2013).

ELGAR, E., *My Friends Pictured Within,* (Novello and Company Limited,n.d.).

GLEADLE, KATHRYN, *British Women in the Nineteenth Century* (Palgrave, 2001).

HERBERT, MARK D., *Ancestral Trails* (Sutton Publishing in conjunction with the Society of Genealogists, 1997).

HODGSON, TERENCE, *The Heart of Colonial Auckland 1865–1910* (Random Century, 1992).

LEACH, PETER AND PEVSNER, NIKOLAUS, *The Buildings of England, Yorkshire West Riding* (Yale University Press, 2009).

MUNDY, SIMON, *Elgar: His life and Times* (Midas Books, 1980).

NORTHROP MOORE, JERROLD, *Spirit of England* (Heinemann, 1984).

——, *A Creative Life* (Oxford University Press: 1987).

ORANGE, CLAUDIA (ed.), *Dictionary of New Zealand Biography, ii* (1940).

RUSHTON, JULIAN, *Elgar, 'Enigma' Variations* (Cambridge University Press: 1999).

STEINBACH, SUSIE, *Women in England, 1760–1914* (Phoenix, 2005).

TAYLOR, SIMON AND GIBSON, KATHRYN, *Manningham, Character and Diversity in a Bradford Suburb* (English Heritage, 2010).

THOMPSON, F. M. L., *The Rise of Respectable Society, A Social History of Victorian Britain, 1830–1900* (Fontana Press: 1988).

LADY TROUBRIDGE, *The Book of Etiquette* (The Associated Bookbuyers' Company, 1926).

VOLLER, LOIS C., *Sentinel at the Gates, Nelson College for Girls, 1883–1983* (Nelson College for Girls, Old Girls' Association, 1983).

WEAVER, CORA, *The Thirteenth Enigma?* (Thames Publishing, 1988).

YOUNG, PERCY, M., *Alice, Enigma of a Victorian Lady* (Dennis Dobson, 1978).

——, *Elgar O. M.* (Collins, 1955).

INDEX

A

Atkins, Ivor 19, 75–6
Atkins, Wulstan E. 9, 11, 24, 42
Auckland (NZ) ix, 47-54, 56-8, 86-90
Awmack, Edwin 6
Awmack, Joseph 6, 28
Awmack, Mary Mercie 5-7, 25, 28 *see also* Weaver, Mary Mercie

B

Baldwyn, Henry 6-7, 47
Baldwyn, Maud 6-7
Box, William 7, 27
Bradford (UK) xiv, 10-11, 15-20, 42-3, 45, 47
Buck, Dr Charles xiii, 9, 22, 27, 70, 76

C

Cheltenham (UK) xiv, 33, 36, 39-40

D

Darell, Edward 34, 39
Darell, Emily 31, 34-5 *see also* Roberts, Emily
Darell, Lucy 34, 38

E

Elgar, Alice 1, 12, 30-9, 41, 57, 61, 73-4, 81, 91 *see also* Roberts, Caroline Alice
Elgar, Ann 10, 23, 27
Elgar, Edward ix, xiii, 1, 3, 5-15, 17, 21-9, 31, 35, 37, 42, 45-6, 52, 56, 63, 70-7, 80-3, 88, 90-1

Elgar Blake, Carice xiv, 10, 15, 17, 36, 39
Exton, Frank 6-7, 9, 27

G

Gilmore, Beatrice 20-1 *see also* Muller, Brünhilde
Grafton, Susannah (Polly) 6, 22, 27, 76, 81, 83
Grey Towers (UK) 79-80, 84
Groveham, Annie xiv, 10-13, 15-16, 42, 45, 90 *see also* Muller, Annie
Groveham, Elizabeth 20, 42-5, 51

H

Hastings (NZ) 56, 66, 68, 85, 87
Hazeldine House, Redmarley (UK) 31-3, 35, 38

L

Leicester, Hubert 9, 27
Leicester, William 9-10, 27
Leipzig (Germany) xiv, 8-13, 21-2, 24
Lygon, Lady Mary 70, 72-7

M

Malone, William G. 65, 78-9, 85
Manningham (UK) 15-18, 20, 43, 45, 47
Mason, Charlotte 44, 49, 51
Muller, Annie 16, 18-21 *see also* Groveham, Annie
Muller, Brünhilde 17, 20-1 *see also* Gilmore, Beatrice
Muller, Ernst Wilhelm Alphonse 16-21
Muller, Ingrid 17, 20

95

Muller, John   17, 20-1
Munro, Helen   56-63, 66—7, 69, 87-90
Munro, John   56-62, 63, 66-8, 85, 87-9
Munro, Joyce   63, 65-9, 87-9
Munro, Kenneth   xiii, 63-5, 67, 78-81, 83-6, 89-90

N

Nelson (NZ)   56, 63-5, 78, 89-90

P

Patea (NZ)   57, 59-63, 65, 67, 79, 86
Pipe, Charlie   7, 13, 24, 26-7
Pipe, Lucy   13, 24, 26-7, 71, 76, 81
Portsmouth and Southsea (UK)   xiv, 34, 38

Q

Quaker   5, 25

R

Raikes, Emma   38
Raikes, Stanley Napier   31-2, 41,
Raikes, William Alves   31-2
Reading (UK)   6, 29, 79
Roberts, Caroline Alice   ix, 31-2, 35, 53, 56, 72 *see also* Elgar, Alice
Roberts, Dora   31, 34-6, 38
Roberts, Emily   34, 36, 38 *see also* Darell, Emily
Roberts, Frederic   32-3, 35, 38, 91
Roberts, Henry Gee   22
Roberts, Julia   31-3
Roberts, Stanley Napier   xiii, 31-41, 90-1
Rodgers, Gipsy   35, 37, 40-1
Roman Catholic   4, 5, 24-27, 34, 38, 47, 81-4, 89, 91

S

Stratford (NZ)   56, 65-8, 78, 85
Surman, Robert   8, 27, 81
Sussman, Alfred   17-18 *see also* Wood Somers, Alfred

T

Trowell, Brian   xiii, 80

U

Unitarian   6, 25, 78

W

Weaver, Ada   1, 4, 6
Weaver, Emily   1, 4
Weaver, Frank   1, 3, 6-8, 10-11, 23, 25, 27, 76, 80-4
Weaver, Frank (Francis) Schubert   82, 84
Weaver, George Bernard Dawson   6, 28-9, 42
Weaver, Helen   xiii, 1, 6-13, 22-5, 28, 42, 44-8, 50-5 *see also* Munro, Helen
Weaver, John (Jack)   82-3
Weaver, Louis   1, 3-4, 6
Weaver, Maria Theresa   10, 81, 83
Weaver, Mary Mercie   6-7 *see also* Awmack, Mary Mercie
Weaver, William   1, 3, 5-7
Wood Somers, Alfred   17-21 *see also* Sussman, Alfred
Worcester (UK)   2-3, 8-10, 13, 22-3, 27, 42, 54, 70, 72, 81-3, 90

Printed in Great Britain
by Amazon